125

The Jet Dragon that Roared

BARRY LLOYD

KEY
Books

HISTORIC COMMERCIAL AIRCRAFT SERIES, VOLUME 11

Front cover image: The dramatic backdrop of Rio de Janeiro overshadows the Raytheon U125A as it prepares for take-off from Santos Dumont, Rio's downtown airport. (Helio Bastos Salmon)

Contents page image: 125 800B VH-SGY, belonging to the Queensland state government, demonstrates its rough field capabilities.

Published by Key Books
An imprint of Key Publishing Ltd
PO Box 100
Stamford
Lincs PE19 1XQ

www.keypublishing.com

The right of Barry Lloyd to be identified as the author of this book has been asserted in accordance with the Copyright, Designs and Patents Act 1988 Sections 77 and 78.

Copyright © Barry Lloyd, 2022

ISBN 978 1 80282 309 7

Typeset by SJmagic DESIGN SERVICES, India.

Contents

Introduction

U nder its various guises, the 125 was produced for 60 years, with more than 1,600 aircraft being completed. While approximately 60 per cent of the aircraft were sold into the North American market, many were sold in Europe, Africa, the former Soviet Union, the Middle East and the Far East, Australasia, and South America. In fact, the aircraft has carried the registrations of more than 60 countries and was in production for longer than any other jet transport aircraft in the world.

The aim of this book is to trace the history of the aircraft from its inception, through the various derivations, until the last aircraft left the factory following the demise of Hawker Beechcraft in 2013. Both the civil and military versions are covered, but there is no attempt to provide more than a general overview, except where individual aircraft are highlighted.

Along with an examination of the various derivations, there are some individual histories, where the aircraft were involved in unusual incidents. Sadly, in more recent years, the 125 has begun to be used increasingly for drug-running, and a few examples of this are examined.

XW930, a Series 1B, seen here at Fairford in 1985, was used for trials by the Royal Aircraft Establishment (RAE) at Bedford and was formerly G-ATPI. (Gerry Manning)

Chapter 1

The Lead-up to Series 1

Following the end of World War Two, the civil aviation situation in Europe was a mess. Generally, only capital cities were served, often just once a day with a flight out in the morning, returning early in the afternoon. Larger companies with interests in continental Europe found this inconvenient, and word reached the designers at de Havilland. The Brabazon Committee, which operated between 1943 and 1945, had called for a type VB – basically an eight-seat aircraft designed to replace the Dragon Rapide biplane. This could be used as a feeder-liner to operate from smaller regional airports. Thus, the Dove, with the design number DH104, was born.

Production of the Dove began 1945, with the first flight taking place on 26 September. The aircraft sold well, with more than 500 being built. Initial production was at de Havilland's Hatfield factory but was moved to Broughton near Chester in 1951, with the last aircraft being produced in 1967. It was particularly appreciated in the US, where its ability to fly into small strips made it attractive to corporate operators. But the emergence of the JetStar and the Sabreliner, albeit initially only with the military, meant that potential operators began to look for speed as well as comfort. The design work on the Dove and its success thus led de Havilland down the road of a successor, this time with jet engines and a more luxurious interior. It's predecessor, the Dove, simply needed seats, but the savvy business jet purchasers were now looking for a more sophicated interior, including a galley.

G-ARYC, the first production 125, is an exhibit at the Mosquito Museum in the UK. (Author)

HB-VAG, a Series 1, was the first 125 to be sold. (David Powell collection)

G-ASSI was the first 125 demonstrator, seen here in the original black and white and later in the full colour publicity photos. (David Powell collection and Bob O'Brien collection)

Series 1B G-ATPB, suffering a wet day in Cologne, was originally owned by Rolls-Royce. (Gerry Manning)

The sales and design teams believed that a more attractive interior would attract corporate customers and the very wealthy. The target was a range of 1,000 miles (1,600km) with about eight seats. The jet engines would offer greater speed, but also use more fuel, so the economics would have to be kept in check. It was recognised that the aircraft would be operated from and to smaller bases where maintenance facilities would not necessarily exist; therefore, reliability and ease of regular maintenance were to be two key factors in the design. The Viper turbojet – manufactured by Armstrong Siddeley, later Bristol Siddeley and, ultimately, Rolls-Royce – was originally designed to power the Jindivik target drone and became the powerplant chosen for the design. As is so often the case, this extremely successful business jet almost didn't see the light of day. The British government's decision to cancel the long-range Blue Streak ballistic missile in April 1960 in favour of the US-built Skybolt, which itself was later cancelled in favour of Polaris, meant there would be no work for de Havilland's talented team of engineers. It was Sir Geoffrey de Havilland himself who declared that with Blue Streak no longer an option, the company should put all its efforts into designing and building a business jet to replace the Dove.

Right: **Next on the register was another Series 1B. G-ATPC was operated by the Civil Aviation Flying Unit in the UK. (Bob O'Brien collection)**

Below: **Group 4 operated this Series 1B, seen here at Staverton in 1983. (Gerry Manning)**

One of the earliest exports to the US was this Series 1A, N1923M. (Richard Vandervord)

G-AWUF was a Series 1B originally operated by MAM Charter. (Bob O'Brien collection)

N151SG, another Series 1A, was sold to the US in 1965. (Gerry Manning)

Right: Parked at the iconic art deco terminal at Liverpool's Speke airport is D-CAFI, a Series 1B. (Bob O'Brien collection)

Below: A view of the production line in 1966, with a Series 1A aircraft in the foreground. This became N125J and was used as a demonstrator. (David Powell collection)

From the outset, fundamental principles were used during the design phase. The fuselage would sit on top of a single wing structure, allowing most of the manufacturing and assembly work to be done separately, before being joined together later in the production process. This was an unusual design principle at the time, which also had the benefit of eliminating the wing spar obstruction in the mid-cabin – a feature of the Dove.

The floor would be slightly recessed, so that the base of the seats was raised on ledges higher than the aisle, thus making the aisle 8in (20cm) lower. The engines would be mounted high on the rear fuselage, thereby reducing the possibility of foreign object damage. Equally, if it became necessary for the aircraft to make a wheels-up landing, any damage would be minimised. An overwing emergency exit hatch was located on the starboard side of the aircraft; on some later versions, overwing hatches were located on both sides of the aircraft.

Two prototypes were built, G-ARYA and G-ARYB. These aircraft had wingspans of 44ft (13.4m) and were 43.5ft (13.26m) long. The first aircraft made its original test flight on 13 August 1962, followed by an appearance at the Farnborough Airshow a month later. On 12 December, the second aircraft made its first flight. Design changes were made to the second prototype, making it more aerodynamically representative of what would become the production aircraft, being fitted out with more equipment. In fact, the production-standard aircraft had a longer fuselage and a larger wingspan. The two prototypes were assembled at de Havilland's Hatfield site, but, as with the Dove, production responsibility was later moved to the Broughton site near Chester.

The airfield first came into existence in the 1930s, when it was known as a 'nearby landing ground' for Royal Air Force (RAF) Sealand and was then known as Bretton, named after the nearby village. The site was chosen during World War Two to be used as a 'shadow factory' – effectively a facility used for assembling aircraft – partly staffed by people with experience of the motor industry, because it was considered to be far enough away from Germany to avoid an air attack. The airfield did not have a paved runway until 1939, and two more were put in place by 1941. It then became known as Hawarden. The site produced the Vickers Wellington and Avro Lancaster bombers, with more than 5,000 being completed, and the airfield retained this name until the Airbus wing assembly plant was built on the airfield, which is nearer to the village of Broughton. On 1 July 1948, de Havilland took over the site, where the Dove, Mosquito and Vampire were built, and it later became more commonly known as Broughton, which is the area to the southeast of the airfield, where Airbus wings are produced today. The entire airfield is contained within Wales. However, the site of the 125 production was, and is, more commonly known as Chester, and this is the name by which it will be referred to throughout this book.

The aircraft went through a considerable number of designation changes during its lifetime, arguably more than most other types ever built, both with the prefix and suffix of series numbers. When de Havilland was taken over by Hawker Siddeley in 1960, it was allowed to operate as a separate company until 1963. Thus, the DH125 became the HS125 until Hawker Siddeley itself became part of British Aerospace in April 1977, when it was nationalised, along with British Aircraft Corporation and Scottish Aviation, to become British Aerospace (BAe). As a result of the merger, the aircraft became known as the BAe 125. For simplicity, the name 125 is used throughout the book, with each chapter highlighting the differences from the previous model.

At this point, it is worth mentioning Harry Hawker, whose name the company carried. Harry George Hawker was born in Australia, but at the age of 22, he decided to migrate to England to become more involved in aviation, arriving in May 1911. In June 1912, he became a mechanic for the Sopwith Aviation Company. He persuaded them to teach him to fly and was able to make his first solo flight after just three lessons. In September 1920, Sopwith Aviation went into liquidation. He later formed a new company, together with Tom Sopwith and others, initially calling it H G Engineering, but it was later renamed

Originally the Hawker Siddeley demonstrator, this Series 1, G-ASSI, was on the Nigerian register for a year before returning to Luton, where it was converted for use as an emergency service trainer nearby. (Richard Vandervord)

Hawker Aircraft in 1933. He died on 12 July 1921, when his Nieuport Goshawk, a single-seat biplane, which had been specifically built as an air racer, crashed while taking off from Hendon aerodrome.

The first production aircraft made its maiden flight on 12 February 1963. It was marketed as the Jet Dragon in recognition of the success of the DH89 Dragon Rapide, but this was soon dropped, and the early models of the aircraft were simply designated DH125 Series 1. In fact, it was not the 125th design, but the 124th. Presumably for reasons of superstition, de Havilland never allocated the design number DH13. Early test flying showed the 125 cabin to be noisy, although none of the aircraft had been fully fitted out as yet. Minor design changes, principally cosmetic ones, were made to reduce the airflow noise. During the Series 1 production run, the number of windows was reduced from six to five; the passenger door was widened, and, in order to accommodate the wider door, the fuselage was lengthened by 12in (30.48cm). The original design called for a T-tail, but following wind-tunnel testing, it was decided that a larger fin would be required. This was fitted above the tail. To allow for future weight growth and improve airfield performance, 18in (45.72cm) was added to the wingspan. In its early days, there were a number of crashes of other types of aircraft with rear engines and a T-tail configuration. Similarly designed aircraft had become locked into a deep stall. Concerned by this, de Havilland carried out almost 4,000 stall tests during flight development, with no failures, but as a precaution, the wing leading edges were fitted with stall strips.

Cabin comfort inside a business jet was obviously a major priority, and during the Comet development, de Havilland had developed a system for pressurising the aircraft using air bled direct from the engines. This system was adapted for use on the 125, with considerable success. The conditioned and temperature-controlled air is then released into the cabin via outlets in the raised floor and by the use of Punkah Louvres® set in the ceiling above the seat, which can be adjusted by the passenger.

The third aircraft, G-ARYC, was first flown on 12 February 1963 and then handed over to Bristol Siddeley on 24 July of that year, for further engine development. Because the 520-Series Viper engine had been developed for military use, a lot of the parts were expendable and many of the engine components had to be redesigned and manufactured with alternative materials. It was only after 1,660 flights and 2,200 hours of flying that certification was eventually achieved, with the type finally receiving its Certificate of Airworthiness (C of A) on 4 June 1964. The first aircraft to receive a

Not a registration that is seen very often, this Zambian Series 1B was photographed while parked at Southend airport, UK. (Richard Vandervord)

An Irish example of a Series 1A is seen on finals to Heathrow. (Richard Vandervord)

Usually 125s are expected to be found in exotic locations, but this aircraft, Series 1A CF-PQG, delivered new in 1965 and operated by Transports et Communications de Québec, found itself in the Canadian winter. The Canadian registration system was changed to C- in 1974 to allow more aircraft to be registered. (Martin Chell)

When first built, this Series 1A aircraft was briefly used as a demonstrator, before being sold to Busy Bee, a Norwegian airline. (Bob O'Brien collection)

certificate was the eighth aircraft to be built, G-ASSI; it was issued on 28 July 1964. The first sale of a 125 was to Chartag, which, as the name suggests, was a charter company, based in Zürich, Switzerland. It was registered HB-VAG and handed over on 2 September 1964. There were a number of other early sales in Europe, but the focus quickly shifted westwards across the Atlantic Ocean. Even in 1964, the US was estimated to be operating thousands of business jets, a number that outstripped the rest of the world combined. It was time to show off the 125 over there, and a demonstrator aircraft, in fact G-ASSI, was suitably fitted out. Demonstration tours are intensive operations, both for the aircraft and those taking part, and this was no exception. 'Gassy', as it was inevitably labelled, left the UK on 7 August 1964 and did not return until 15 November. During that time, it had logged more than 500 hours during 105 days in 32 US states, together with six Canadian provinces. Throughout this time, the aircraft performed very impressively. While of itself, 500 hours might not seem like a lot of flying, it should be considered that some business jets do not accumulate that many flying hours in a year.

This is an appropriate moment to mention the competitor aircraft that were available at the time, most of which were from US manufacturers. The first of these was the Lockheed JetStar, fitted with four engines and built at a time when fuel was incredibly cheap. More fuel-efficient engines were fitted later in its life. The aircraft was produced between 1961 and 1978. A number of them are preserved around North America, perhaps the most famous being the one owned by Elvis Presley, N777EP, which is on display at his former home, Graceland, in Memphis, Tennessee. A total of 205 aircraft were built. The second business jet in operation around this time was the North American, later Rockwell, Sabreliner. Built primarily for the military market and used extensively by the US Air Force, the aircraft was available to civilian operators between 1963 and 1983. Both aircraft were originally fitted with the Pratt & Whitney JT12 turbojet engine, but in the case of the Sabreliner, they were normally replaced later with the Garrett TFE731. As with the JetStar, a number of aircraft are preserved throughout North America. A total of 485 aircraft were sold in the civil market.

Israel Aerospace Industries (IAI) built the Westwind between 1965 and 1987. It was originally designed in the US by a company known as Aero Commander and was known as the Jet Commander. The low-slung fuselage is reminiscent of its propeller-driven cousin of the same name. In 1965, the Aero Commander company was acquired by Rockwell, but since it already manufactured the Sabreliner, and because of US antitrust laws, it was not allowed to keep both aircraft in production. The manufacturing rights to the Westwind were sold to IAI in 1968. Despite its somewhat ungainly appearance, the aircraft could be fitted with up to ten seats, a factor that may have contributed to its success, with almost 300 aircraft sold.

Probably the biggest straight competitor to the 125 worldwide was the Dassault Falcon 20. This aircraft was in production between 1965 and 1988, and more than 500 were built. It established Dassault firmly as a business jet manufacturer, its previous designs having been fighter jets, such as the Étendard and Mirage. It has now been succeeded by the Falcon 2000 and other larger variants. Whenever business jets are mentioned, especially in the US, the name 'Lear' is never far from peoples' lips, possibly because it was the first choice for many Hollywood film stars. Bill Lear set up his own company to design an entry-level business jet for the market, and it was introduced in 1964 as the Lear 23 and underwent subsequent improvements, becoming the Lear 24. More than 259 Lear 20 Series were built, and, as with the JetStar and Sabreliner, a number are preserved in the US. More than 300 of both types were produced between 1966 and 1979.

Despite the local competition, orders quickly followed, and such was the enthusiasm for the aircraft that a dealership was set up in North America. One lesson that had been learnt with the Dove was that the lack of adequate support for the aircraft had damaged its sales prospects in the region, and de Havilland was determined that this would not happen again. The orders for 20 aircraft following the sales tour spurred the design team at Hatfield to greater efforts, realising that improvements would need to be made to the Series 1 in order to make it more acceptable to the market. As a result of this, only eight aircraft of the original Series 1 were ever built. The name 'Jet Dragon', which had been used as a marketing name at the development stage, was dropped in favour of calling it by its design number. The US market was generally more used to numerical designations, plus the name would not necessarily translate easily into other languages. As part of the marketing effort, de Havilland had discussed a deal with Pan American Airways. Colonel Charles Lindbergh, on behalf of Pan American, had visited de Havilland even before the 125 had flown and was keen to set up a business jets division, both as an operator and a sales agent for the aircraft in the US. There were a number of meetings and discussions, but it became apparent that Pan American was looking for a larger, more sophisticated aircraft. As part of a potential deal, an offer was made by de Havilland to retrofit the 125 with a General Electric CF-700 engine, the same engines that were fitted to the competitor Falcon 20. However, that would mean de Havilland would be unable to guarantee the range of the aircraft, plus there would, of course, be the inevitable delay while new design drawings were produced. Pan American decided that this did not fit with its expectations and instead turned its attention to a major competitor of the 125, the Dassault Falcon 20. Following this, de Havilland identified a number of North American distributors. These were Atlantic Aviation Sales, based in Wilmington, Delaware, and AiResearch Aviation Services, based in Los Angeles. Canada was represented by Timmins Aviation, which later became Atlantic Aviation and subsequently Innotech; its headquarters was in Montreal.

Production was now divided into two groups. These now carried an 'A' or 'B' suffix, with 'A' representing those destined for the North American market and 'B' representing the rest of the world. The first aircraft to be delivered under the new scheme was originally registered as G-ASSJ, and then changed to N125J once it had been registered in the US. This aircraft was delivered to Atlantic Aviation Services in September 1964. As part of the fresh marketing initiative and reflecting the changes that were taking place in the British aviation industry at the time, the designation was changed to Hawker Siddeley 125, but the original name of de Havilland was already too widely known and respected for it to be easily erased. The aircraft was now designated as the Series 1A. A decision had been taken by de Havilland's management that it would be more beneficial in terms of both cost and materials available to part-complete the aircraft in Chester and then fly them to the US for interior completion. The aircraft that were ordered for the North American market would normally leave Chester in the green zinc chromate primer paint, which is designed to prevent corrosion of the aluminium body. Interior furnishings would then be chosen by the purchaser and fitted by the dealership. Despite the relative modernity of the onboard equipment, there was one invaluable item that was carried on every trip: the passenger door would later be fitted with a set of integral steps, thus allowing the passengers an elegant entry and exit to and from the aircraft. However, there was no such luxury for the ferry pilots, who would carry a large wooden box with rope handles on every flight. Not only did the box serve as a receptacle for any tools that might be required, but also as a means of entering and leaving the aircraft safely, particularly at intermediate refuelling stops. This was classed as an essential item and was returned to the factory after every trip. Additionally, secondary avionics would be carried, to deal with the long northern flights because, at that time, there were fewer navigational aids. Typical range for the early 125s was about 1,000 miles (1,852km), so several stops would be required during the ferry flights. The routing would normally take the aircraft via Iceland, Greenland, and northeastern Canada, depending on the weather conditions at the time.

Busy Bee took delivery of this aircraft in March 1968. It was the first of three aircraft operated by the airline, which ceased operating in 1992. (Martin Chell)

This Series 1B was, for a time, owned by the company that also owned G-LORI, whose adventures are described in Chapter 10. (Martin Chell)

Chapter 2

Series 2 and 3

With an established network set up in the US, and sales in the rest of the world beginning to appear, de Havilland now turned its attention to how the 125 could be improved. It was stopped in its tracks though, by an unexpected development. The RAF, now equipped with jet fighters such as the Vampire and the Meteor, needed a platform on which to train navigators for fast jets. From the 1950s, the aircraft of choice for this programme had been the Valetta or the Varsity, both military versions of the Vickers Viking. Although there was sufficient space within the aircraft for a classroom, the problem was that being piston-engined propeller aircraft, they could not even begin to match the speed of the jets, thus the navigational training completed in the Valettas and Varsities was compromised once the training was put into practice in a much faster aircraft.

There was a defined need by the RAF for a new aircraft, but what could that be? There would never be enough money in the defence budget for an aircraft designed specifically for training navigators, so some sort of compromise would have to be reached. The RAF had heard rumours of what was described as a 'jet-propelled Dove replacement' and was keen to find out more. Having then looked carefully at the 125, the RAF decided that it was exactly what it wanted. This was rare praise indeed, because the usual procedure with these sorts of procurements is that the Ministry of Defence and the operators immediately want to change the manufacturer's specification to the point where it is almost a different aircraft and then grumble when the manufacturer explains this will result in a considerable increase in price and a delay in delivery.

The RAF had a requirement for 20 aircraft, and it was this potential business that had further convinced the board of de Havilland to go ahead with the programme, since such an order would now comprise two-thirds of the original commitment. The contract negotiations began in September 1962, although such is the way of government procurement contracts that the final details were not completed until April 1964. The first of the 20 made its maiden flight in December 1964 and was delivered to the RAF on 30 March 1965, with the final aircraft being delivered in mid-1966.

The aircraft was identical in appearance to the civil version, the only significant difference being that the engines fitted to this series were the Viper Mk 301. Another small difference was that there were only four windows on each side instead of the traditional six, since this was where the electronic equipment racks were fitted. The arrangement allowed for two navigator trainees to sit side-by-side in rearward-facing seats. Once delivered, the aircraft were quickly put into service. The fleet was split between two principal training units, with six going into service with No. 1 Air Navigational School (ANS), based at that time at RAF Manby in Lincolnshire, and 13 going to RAF Stradishall in Suffolk. The remaining aircraft was delivered to the Royal Aircraft Establishment (RAE) at Farnborough for trials.

Later, all flying training, with the exception of pilot training, was moved to RAF Finningley in Yorkshire; this included No. 1 ANS. Following this, a standard RAF colour scheme for all training aircraft was introduced, starting with the 125, which would replace the familiar silver and orange Day-Glo scheme that the aircraft had previously worn. The new scheme consisted of a white top with a bare metal underside. A red cheat line separated the two, complemented by a white radome and a matt black anti-glare panel on the nose. From its introduction into service, it was designated the 'Dominie', a term derived from the Scottish word for a schoolmaster. In 'de Havilland speak' it was known as the Series 2. As the Dominie entered service, so did the V-bombers, which had been designed during the height of the

XS711 was one of 20 aircraft ordered by the RAF for training purposes and called the Dominie. (Bob O'Brien collection)

XS728 takes off from Greenham Common on a training mission. Note the reduced number of windows. (Richard Vandervord)

Two members of the crew in discussion while XS733 is on display at RAF Leuchars in 1976. (Gerry Manning)

RAF Valley is where Dominie XS736 is seen parked during a visit there. (David Powell collection)

Above: Seen here at Fairford, XS739 was one of the last Dominie T1s to be retired from service. The legend celebrates 64 years of flying training. (Richard Vandervord)

Left: Here is c/n 25062, seen during assembly at Chester. This Series 3B went on to become VH-ECE. (David Powell collection)

Cold War to respond to any potential aggression from the Soviet Union. Naturally, it was important to have accurate navigation for this task, and the most important training was conducted with this in mind.

During this time, several modifications were made to the training systems installed on the aircraft, with each aircraft passing through Marshall's of Cambridge for the refit. Following this, they were then reallocated to No. 3 Flying Training School, which, by then, had been relocated to RAF Cranwell in Lincolnshire. Another new colour scheme was applied, this time consisting of a black overall fuselage, with a white roof, but this took place during the period when the aircraft were going through the avionics upgrade.

On 19 October 2010, the government announced its Strategic Defence and Security Review, which cut a swathe through the existing aircraft capability. The new perception was about single-seat capability, and so the Tornado and the Nimrod were to become things of the past. By extension, the reduced requirement for navigators, now designated as 'weapons systems officers', meant the

Right: VH-ECE, seen here at Singapore in 1967, was one of two aircraft operated by Qantas for crew training. (Bob O'Brien collection)

Below: This aircraft, a Series 3B, would have been the smallest aircraft operated by Court Line. It was later owned by Shell Aviation. (Bob O'Brien collection)

This appropriately registered Series 3B only carried the company's colours for just over a year. (Richard Vandervord)

An interesting line-up at Heathrow, from the days when business jets were based there, with G-TAZN (Series 3A) nearest the camera, together with G-BAYT (-600B) and G-BACI (-400A) in the group. (Richard Vandervord)

For two years, Series 3B G-AVAI was the Hawker Siddeley demonstrator. The flags of the countries it visited are shown on the lower cheat line. (Bob O'Brien collection)

Ferranti, the owner of this Series 3B/RA, was a large electrical company that went bankrupt in 1993. (Richard Vandervord)

need for the Dominies also diminished. It was decided to retire the aircraft in January 2011, and the Cranwell-based squadron, having had a close relationship with the Dominie, decided to retire the aircraft in style, with a series of flypasts around the country, culminating in a finale at their base. The type had served the RAF well for an amazing 45 years, and all those who had been associated with them remembered them fondly. Several examples were preserved and can be found at the RAF Museum at Cosford, the Newark Air Museum and Cotswold (Kemble) Airport.

While all this was taking place, the civil side of the business at Chester was not being ignored. From the very beginning, it was noted that there were differences between the airworthiness requirements for aircraft to be registered with the US Federal Aviation Administration (FAA) aircraft and those for the rest of the world. The principal differences revolved around systems, equipment and avionics. 'A' aircraft used an air-conditioning system manufactured by AiResearch, while a Hawker Siddeley Dynamics package was installed in the 'B' aircraft. Other differences involved the use of US-manufactured radio, radar and navigational aids. Continuous development was taking place with the engine too, with a more powerful version of the Viper becoming available. This was designated 522 and allowed the aircraft to become heavier without sacrificing performance. The change of engine resulted in it being designated as a Series 3B. The first aircraft to be fitted with this engine were two ordered by Qantas for crew training. These were registered as VH-ECE and VH-ECF. In fact, the 3B was developed to Qantas's specifications, with the flight deck layout being adapted to appear similar to that of the Boeing 707. VH-ECF was sold back to the UK, but VH-ECE continued to fly with Qantas and by 1980 had accumulated 13,000 hours flight time and 50,000 landings. When it was finally retired in May 1981, having been delivered in September 1964, it had achieved 13,926 hours and 53,882 landings. The engines were removed from the aircraft and sold to Rolls-Royce and the airframe was sold to a Qantas flight engineer in October 1981 and transported to The Oaks, a private grass airfield southwest of Sydney, where it is now believed to be in a derelict condition. A second 3B, VH-CAO, formerly owned by the Department of Civil Aviation, is also stored at the site. The second aircraft, VH-ECF, took part in the England to Australia Air Race on 1 and 2 January 1970, winning the executive jet category award. It was later bought by McAlpine Aviation and stayed on the British

G-AVXL was a Series 3B, which was operated by McAlpine, an FBO (fixed-base operator) based at Luton, near London. (Richard Vandervord)

Left: Seen here parked at Lima's Jorge Chavez Airport is Series 3A/RA N125F. (Gerry Manning)

Below: Not many 125s found their way to Indonesia. This Series 3B/RA was owned by Pelita Air Service, the aviation division of Indonesia's national oil company. (Richard Vandervord)

Right: The ill-fated Series 3B, G-AVGW, which crashed at Luton during a training flight. (Ken Haynes)

Below: VR-BGD was an early example of a business jet being registered in Bermuda. The aircraft was a Series 3B/RA, owned by Air Hanson, but based in the UK. (Richard Vandervord)

This was a Series 3B/RC operated as a communications aircraft by the Brazilian Air Force. (Richard Vandervord)

This Series 3B aircraft was operated by the Australian Department of Civil Aviation. (Bob O'Brien collection)

Above: Series 3B G-AZVS was operated by both Eastern Airways and Beecham Pharmaceutical Co. (Bob O'Brien collection)

Left: Classed as a Series 3B/RC, and pictured in Miami, VC93-2120 was operated as a communications aircraft. (Gerry Manning)

One of the early Nigerian customers' Series 3Bs, delivered in 1967. (Gerry Manning)

register, but it crashed and was written off in an accident near Colombia Regional Airport in Missouri on 30 January 1990 while operating for a company called Slender You (UK) Ltd and registered as G-OBOB.

It seems that whenever a basic aircraft design is deemed to be successful, there is no limit to the number of ideas for converting the aircraft to other uses, and the 125 was no exception. There were two ideas considered, one of which was a communications aircraft for the Royal Navy, and the other a somewhat bizarre arrangement to turn it into an anti-submarine warfare aircraft, involving a rotodome placed on top of the fuselage, which then necessitated a twin-finned tail assembly. The work would have been undertaken by the Hawker Siddeley factory at Brough near Kingston-Upon-Hull, home of the Beverley and the Buccaneer. Despite a considerable amount of design work being completed, however, the idea was eventually dropped. Other special variants were produced though, including what was known on the drawing board as the HS125 Protector, a maritime patrol aircraft equipped with a search radar and cameras. Other variants are dealt with later in the book.

While all this was taking place, one important development being incorporated into the aircraft was increased range. The models with the new design were designated as Series 3A/RA and 3B/RA, with the RA standing for 'range added'. Other design features, such as the addition of mainwheel door housing, reduced drag and increased the cruising speed slightly, although, in many cases, the benefit was also reduced fuel consumption. Based on these improvements, a tour of Latin America was undertaken, using G-AVRG. This was no easy task, because whenever a demonstration tour is put together, the potential customers invariably want to see the aircraft in the most trying of conditions. During this demo tour, the aircraft made 95 demonstration flights in 15 different countries, in temperatures of up to 40°C and at airfields with elevations up to 9,000ft (2,743m).

Demo tours are, of course, expensive undertakings, but invariably result in orders, and this one was no exception. An order from the Brazilian Air Force (FAB) quickly followed for five aircraft. These were designated Series 3B/RCs, the RC in this case signifying a slight increase in the zero weight (ZFW) and maximum take-off weight (MTOW), respectively, of this variant. This was done to cope with the often-shorter runways and the need for the maximum possible range. The crew and aircraft having survived the rigours of the South American tour, it was time to take the aircraft in the opposite direction, to Asia. This time, the tour was to last for 87 days. The airfields were equally challenging, with the aircraft frequently operating from what were little more than unpaved strips – often just sand with a thin layer of grass on top which, depending on whether it had rained or not, were either slippery or, if dry, the take-off run would have to be increased. Aircraft designers tend to think of all

This Series 3B aircraft was originally delivered to Imperial Chemical Industries of the UK in October 1969. (Martin Chell)

N345DA was built as a Series 3A in 1966. It eventually became SX-BSS. (Martin Chell)

the possibilities in terms of both safety and comfort when designing a business jet, and the people at de Havilland were no exception. However, one thing that does not immediately come to mind as you look up from your drawing board to the rain running down the windows on a cold winter's day in the northern hemisphere is that other countries have consistently warmer and more humid climates. During the demo tour, it was quickly realised that the aircraft needed an auxiliary power unit (APU) to provide enough power to keep the air conditioning running during turnarounds in hotter climes. The APU would keep the cabin cooler and drier than the air outside, which was particularly important when the aircraft was on the ground for considerable periods between flights.

By now it was time for 'Romeo Golf' to move on, and in August 1971, it was sold to Court Line, which kept it for four years before selling it on to Shell Oil Company. Rather like a car showroom, once the demonstrator has done its job, it is time to sell it on and use a newer model. Naturally, being an aircraft with a lot of hours and landings on the clock, it is sold at a discount. This has two advantages: it introduces a new customer into the market, and because the aircraft has aided the sales and marketing effort during the demo tours, it has thus proved itself. From a technical point of view, with the demo tours being so intense, the aircraft is being heavily used on a daily basis, and this can often highlight issues that can be improved on future designs, the addition of the APU being a classic example of something that would not normally come to light during its working life as an executive jet.

Chapter 3

The -400

By 1968, more than 140 125s had been sold. The largest proportion of these was to the US, with no less than 85 making the transatlantic crossing. Of the remaining export sales, 31 had been sold as 'B' Series. In a sense, the 125 was now becoming a victim of its own success. Early customers, happy with the aircraft's overall performance, were now coming back and asking if there was a newer model to be had. The short answer was no. The 125 had been a private venture from the beginning, and while capital had been put back into development, there was insufficient funds to invest in significant new improvements. The board would have to be convinced that the investment was worthwhile, and this is never an easy thing to do. Along with this obstacle, Rolls-Royce, which by now held overall responsibility for the Viper engine, had said that it could no longer offer any improvements to it. Additionally, there was a feeling that the 125 exterior design needed modernising to at least keep it level with its competitors. Thus, what would normally have been called the Series 4 was now changed to the Series 400 – a purely cosmetic marketing tool to increase sales, especially in North America. With the board finally convinced that it was that right thing to do, the design department set about the improvements. One of the more major of these was the design of the entrance door. The plug-type upward-sliding door, which had been fitted to the aircraft since day one, was now replaced by an outward-opening door, which, as well as being easy to operate, could now incorporate a set of four steps, making the aircraft completely independent of ground servicing. The door width, now considered excessive at 36in (91cm), was reduced to 27in (69cm). The Series 400 was also treated to improved cabin noise insulation – always a welcome development.

GEC-Marconi was the only owner of this -403B version, which it operated for more than 20 years. (Gerry Manning)

G-AYER was owned by the Rank Organisation, an entertainment company in the UK. This aircraft was a -400F. (Richard Vandervord)

G-AYOJ was the allocated registration for this -403B. It is seen here outside the factory at Chester. This aircraft became G-LORI, which is the subject of a story in Chapter 10. (Ken Haynes)

The new model was first announced at the 1968 Farnborough Airshow, with the first example making is appearance at the highly prestigious National Business Aircraft Association (NBAA) show, whose base rotates annually around the US. In October 1968, it was the turn of Houston. The aircraft displayed, N125J, contained yet further improvements, such as a higher MTOW. The cockpit had not been forgotten either, with more comfortable pilot's seats, and the main instrument panel and the central pedestal being made more ergonomic. The fact there was no immediate upgrade for the Viper 522 was less of a problem than had been expected, with the engine having achieved a level of reliability such that its time between overhauls was now 1,600 hours.

The year 1968 turned out to be a very significant one for the 125. A total of 50 aircraft were sold. One of the early customers was the South African Air Force, which bought them primarily as VIP transports and named them Mercurius after the Roman messenger god, but, in fact, they were fitted with rails to launch underwing rockets. Although a total of seven aircraft were delivered, the order was never officially announced.

A further military application for the 125 was taken up by the Argentinian Navy. They had ordered a Series 400, which was delivered in 1972, essentially as a VIP transport. It was given the serial 5-T-30 and operated normally until the outbreak of the Falklands (Malvinas) War in 1982. At that point, the Escuadrón Fénix had been formed with the intention of flying support and communications missions; the aircraft was given a new serial number, 0653, but was in fact being used as a navigation aircraft for the IAI-built Daggers and Douglas Skyhawks, and also to act as a decoy, drawing away the Sea

One of a few 125s that appeared on the Italian register, I-GJBO was a -400B. It is seen here parked in a remote corner of Zürich Airport. (Gerry Manning)

The Maersk Shipping Company was an early customer for the -400A and operated the aircraft for 13 years. The registration has since been used on two other aircraft. (Richard Vandervord)

Hangared in Paraguay's capital, Asunción, is ZP-TDF, a -400A. This aircraft has now been re-registered as ZP-TKO. (Gerry Manning)

The 200th 125 leaves the production line at Chester. This -400A was later operated by the Brazilian Air Force. (David Powell collection)

This -400B aircraft, EU 93-2119, was operated by the Brazilian Air Force for 30 years as a calibration aircraft, only being withdrawn from use in 2004. (Martin Chell)

Harriers. A further assignment was to relay messages between the Argentinian command post at Port Stanley and low-flying Argentinean attack aircraft. Following the war, the aircraft was withdrawn from use and later sold as LV-AXZ to an Argentinian homeware company called Alparamis in 1987.

One side effect of the increasing orders for the 125 was that Beech Aircraft Corporation, based in Wichita, Kansas, began to take an interest in the aircraft. It had wanted to break into the executive jet market for some time and had even considered putting jet engines on a King Air, their twin-engined propeller-driven executive aircraft, typically fitted with seven seats. Having an established type was clearly preferable, and discussions began to take place between the two manufacturers. So it was that in December 1969 a formal agreement was announced. Beech now replaced Atlantic Aviation of Canada (previously Timmins) as agents for the aircraft, and AiResearch in the US now became responsible for all sales in North America. As part of this remarketing, the 125 would now be known as the BH-125 and Beech would purchase 40 'green' aircraft, which would be completed to local customer requirements. In a separate agreement was a plan to produce two derivatives of the 125. One, the BH-600, was planned to be a larger and faster version of the standard aircraft. The second, designated BH-200, would be an entirely new design – newer, smaller and with the ability to operate from short runways. In fact, de Havilland had taken such a design to the drawing board and designated it the DH135, but this had never been followed up.

One result of the agreement with Beech was the souring of the relationship with the other dealers in North America, but it would have been difficult for Hawker Siddeley to turn down an order for 40 aircraft and the possibilities that the deal with Beech offered for future sales. It is very often the case that operators of a large twin-engined aircraft, such as the King Air, will look to upgrade to a mid-sized jet for their next acquisition. The reality, however, was somewhat different. Post-1969, the sales of business jets hit a low point, and not all the initial batch of 40 were sold. The work on the BH-600 continued, but as it progressed, it became apparent that a joint operation was never going to work. There were many differences between the ways the companies operated, the most fundamental of which were design practices. The arrangement became untenable and the BH-200 programme itself only reached the brochure stage, with a wooden mock-up being put together in Hatfield. The agreement was formerly dissolved in September 1975.

One month later at the NBAA show in New Orleans, Hawker Siddeley announced it had set up its own US marketing department, based in Washington. This organisation would be responsible for sales within the US and also to Mexico. Canadian sales would revert to Timmins, which now operated under the name Innotech Aviation.

Retrofits – the F-Series

As more fuel-efficient engines became available, coupled with the ever-increasing price of fuel, the idea of retrofitting more modern fan engines to existing aircraft became increasingly more attractive. Starting in 1981, a number of operators asked if it would be possible to fit the new quieter, more fuel-efficient Garrett engines. At that time, the TFE700 was selling well and the designers at BAe, as it had then become, began to produce drawings for the retrofitted aircraft. To prove the point, they took G-BFAN, a -400B Series aircraft that had been built in 1971 and later converted to a -600, and used this as the prototype for the -400F retrofit.

The conversion would not work for the very early series, primarily because the systems would have been incompatible with the cabin pressurisation systems originally produced by Hawker Siddeley Dynamics. Apart from this, the retrofit costs for the aircraft concerned would have greatly exceeded their resale value. Those aircraft that had been fitted with the Garrett AiResearch cabin systems were eminently suitable though, and many operators, who were happy with the aircraft overall, jumped at the chance to have them re-engined. Not least of the considerations was that it was cheaper than buying a new -700 Series, and this had not gone unnoticed by BAe, but the strong sales of the -700 served to quell their fears, plus there was always a good chance that an operator who had the F-series conversion would come back later for a new model. The F-series, with the Garrett engine fitted, was able to give an increase in range of 50 per cent over the previous powerplants.

There was more to the retrofit than just changing engines, however, and it was decided that such work could only be undertaken by BAe at the Chester factory or, in the case of the 'A' models, at AiResearch's facility in Los Angeles. Thus, a formal agreement was put in place, whereby AiResearch alone would deal with 'A' Series conversions and the 'B' Series would be handled by BAe at Chester. There were two exceptions. Two aircraft, originally owned by Garrett – a Series 1A and a -400A – were brought to Chester for the work to be done and the certification process to take place. Subsequent certification was issued by the FAA in February 1979.

When major conversion work is being carried out, it presents an opportunity to do other work on the aircraft, and many operators took the chance to fit newer radios and navigation aids, and often a new cabin trim. Performance guarantees had been given by BAe with the retrofit, but, in fact, these were exceeded in most cases. Some of the range increases – calculated at 50 per cent in service – turned out, in some cases, to be as much as 70 per cent. A useful attribute, especially for the North American operators.

With the design drawings finalised and in the hands of AiResearch, 48 aircraft had been booked for the retrofit process by February 1981. Indeed, such was the demand for used 125s to undergo the procedure that it became almost impossible to find a used -400 in the US. In the meantime, the RAF, which had been operating a fleet of six earlier 125s, took the decision to re-engine them all. Thus, the -400s became CC. Mk 1A, and the -600s CC. Mk 2A. The process continued apace, and by September 1981, the total number of retrofits had reached 65. Mindful of the demand for the F-400, BAe then began to offer the retrofitted models alongside its new aircraft, the theory being that customers that could not afford a new aircraft and were wary of buying an older one, could now be offered a fully refurbished interim model from the Chester factory. Such was the demand for new -700s at the time, that delivery dates were slipping further

Supplied as a -400A, this aircraft saw 24 years' service. Here, N125CW sits on the parking area at Washington National Airport in this 1989 photograph. It was broken up in 1991. (Gerry Manning)

and further down the calendar, whereas the F-400 could be delivered in a shorter timescale. BAe was so confident in the new series that G-BFAN, noted earlier as the first aircraft to be converted, was used for many years as the shuttle aircraft around the BAe factories, including a regular run to Toulouse, acquiring thousands of hours flying time in the process – something rather unusual for a corporate jet. The aircraft, after having several different owners, was finally sold to the Democratic Republic of the Congo, but its current fate is unknown. It had been in service with BAe for 24 years when it was sold.

The Mexican government was the first operator of this -400A. The dual registrations suggest it was also used by the Mexican Air Force. The same registrations were later applied to a Sabreliner. (Richard Vandervord)

The South African Air Force operated a total of seven -400Bs, of which this was the last to be delivered. (Martin Chell)

Chapter 4

The -600

With the Beech debacle now firmly in the past, Hawker Siddeley set about the next stage of improvements for the 125. There has long been a technical disconnect between airframe and engine manufacturers. Airframe manufacturers are constantly looking for a better (more efficient and more powerful) engine, while the engine manufacturers, having produced what they consider to be a perfectly acceptable product, are irked by the airframe manufacturers' constant requests for performance improvements. So it was with the 125. Rolls-Royce had developed the Mk 600 Series of Viper engines, which promised an increase in power. The Viper engine was a turbojet, but by the late 1960s this model of powerplant was becoming increasingly obsolete, driven by increasing fuel prices and the latest engine developments. The era of large jet transport aircraft had now arrived, for which the turbofan (or bypass in Rolls-Royce parlance) was now the engine design of choice. This modern design, irrespective of which side of the Atlantic it was produced, offered a substantial reduction in fuel burn, together with a significant reduction in noise. The exponential increase in air travel, which had begun in the late 1960s, meant increased noise for those who lived near airports, and people were becoming increasingly conscious of this, leading the certification authorities to take a greater interest in noise levels.

Unfortunately for Rolls-Royce and the Viper, tests showed that the Mk 600 would be even noisier than the Mk 500 Series. In collaboration with Fiat of Italy, a considerable amount of work was done on the Viper, resulting in an engine designated the '601'. Some thought was given to fitting this engine on the Series 400 airframe and designating it the '125-500', but the few benefits were outweighed by the

For a number of years, this aircraft, a -600A, was owned by British Aerospace (BAe). In this case, it was leased to the government of Kuwait and is seen here at Heathrow in June 1978. (Gerry Manning)

G-AZHS was the second prototype Series 600, which was in fact converted during production from a -400. (David Powell collection)

development costs. In fact, the resulting aircraft would have been useful only for those operators that frequented hot and high airfields, but these were very much in the minority and the idea was dropped.

Apart from the decision over a suitable engine for the -600, a number of other developments were taking place. Customers had asked for a larger cabin and increased range, both of which would require a different engine. The fuselage was lengthened by 24in (61cm) by the use of a 'plug' forward of the wing/fuselage fairing. This allowed an additional window on each side, thus restoring the overall appearance to that seen on the early Series 1s. Other improvements included the redesign of the cockpit fairing, and a reprofile of the pressurised portion of the fuselage to minimise drag. The radome was extended, together with the dorsal fin, as part of a strengthening of the tail in order to cope with the overall increases in weight. This also necessitated the strengthening of the main undercarriage. A further innovation was the incorporation of a 50-gal (227-lit) fuel tank into the dorsal fin above the rear fuselage. Although the Viper 601 was a long and narrow engine, this was less apparent on the -600 and the fairing was designed with this in mind and was also capable of having a silencer fitted. This was obviously becoming a quite different model from its predecessors. The problem of noise had not gone away, however; if anything, it was receiving more attention than ever, especially from governments. The US was the first to introduce firm legislation in 1974, with the UK following in 1976. Initially, the legislation applied only to new aircraft, but it was clear that, over time, all aircraft would have to comply. Since the inception of the jet engine, Rolls-Royce had undertaken studies into the noise emissions from jet engines but had not been required to contain it in any way. Now the time had come, and a new word came into the aviation vocabulary: 'hush kits.' In the case of the Viper, this took the form of a nozzle divided into eight lobes, similar to that which had been added to the Avon engines of the de Havilland Comet.

The combination of a new engine and improved aerodynamics meant that a full payload – six passengers, plus baggage, plus full fuel reserves – could now be carried for 1,570nm (2,907km), enough

A view of the -600 production line at Chester. (David Powell collection)

This was the Hawker Siddeley -600 demonstrator, which sadly crashed at Dunsfold in November 1975. The full details are in Chapter 10. (Ken Haynes)

An air-to-air shot of G-AYBH, a -400 that was converted during production to a -600. It went to the Philippines and later to the Irish Air Corps. It was written off following an accident at the corps' headquarters in Baldonnel on 21 November 1979. (David Powell collection)

Probably the only 125 to appear on the Nicaraguan register, this -600 Series carries the old registration prefix. It was later changed to 'YN-'. (Richard Vandervord)

The registration is an additional pointer to the fact that Rolls-Royce was the owner of this -600B. It was delivered in 1973. (Richard Vandervord)

Unusually, this registration was used twice for a 125. J. C. Bamford (JBC), a manufacturer of construction equipment, took delivery of this -600A in 1976, having previously leased a -600 fan version in 1973. (Richard Vandervord)

This was the last of 13 different registrations that this aircraft wore during its lifetime. Note the different font for the 'RD' suffix. It was previously N514MH and originally destined for display at California City Airport, which, despite its name, lies in the desert 100 miles (160km) north of Los Angeles, but was dumped with other aircraft withdrawn from use. It was first delivered as a -600A in 1974. (David Hedges)

In the days when the 'YU-' prefix was allocated to Yugoslavia, this -600B is seen visiting Heathrow. It was owned by the Yugoslav National Oil Corporation. The 'YU-' prefix now only applies to Serbia. (Richard Vandervord)

to allow it to fly coast-to-coast in the US with just one stop – an important selling point. Nevertheless, the target was always for a non-stop coast-to-coast range, something that was already achievable by one of the 125's rivals, the Gulfstream II. The aircraft was significantly larger and more expensive than the 125, but the French manufacturer Dassault was building a prototype of the Falcon 50, too, which would also be capable of the coast-to-coast operation.

An unexpected and certainly unwanted development in this progress was the bankruptcy of Rolls-Royce in 1971. Two of the Series 400 airframes had been taken off the production line with the intention of making them into Series 600 prototypes, equipped with the Viper 601 engines. The first aircraft selected was registered as G-AYBH, and it first flew on 21 January 1971. The second aircraft, subsequently registered as G-AZHS, became a victim of the bankruptcy. Rolls-Royce was building the RB 211 turbofan engine specifically for commercial airliners, but the development phase had not been without its problems, which had forced the engine manufacturer into bankruptcy. The strategic importance of Rolls-Royce, not least to Britain, was that it supplied the engines for most of the country's military aircraft; as such, the government had to take control of the company and nationalise it. The short-term effect of this was the voiding of all previous contracts; thus, no new engines could be supplied until new contracts had been completed and signed. This meant the first flight of G-AZHS did not take place until more than ten months later, on 25 November 1971. Despite this setback, the board of Hawker Siddeley remained confident in the future of its executive jet and authorised the manufacture of 38 Series 600s. At that time though, there was something of a slump in markets worldwide, and initial sales were difficult to achieve. One bright light in this was an order from the RAF, which purchased two aircraft, designating them CC Mk 2s. These were allocated to No. 32 (The Royal) Squadron, based at RAF Northolt, northwest of London. They would be used for executive flights, specifically for members of the government, visiting dignitaries and, from time to time, the royal family.

It was not only as an executive transport that government agencies ordered the aircraft though. In Germany, the Bundesanstalt für Flugsicherung (BFS), the German agency responsible for air traffic control, ordered a -600 Series. In fact, the BFS had been good customers for British aircraft, with a fleet of Doves and Avro 748s already at its disposal. The 125-600 was required specifically to monitor the

Left: Delivered new to the United Arab Emirates in 1977, this -600B had several owners and was last heard of in Venezuela. (Richard Vandervord)

Below: There is no doubt who is the owner of this aircraft. This -600A was bought in December 1989 by a fast-food company based in Miami. (Martin Chell)

higher levels of the airways, which were now being used increasingly by jet aircraft. This version had a maximum ceiling of 45,000ft (13,700m). The internal equipment designed to monitor both civil and military navigation aids was mounted on rails, so that the aircraft could quickly be converted to carry VIPs, if required. This was constructor's number (c/n) 256053, D-CFSK. Another unusual use to which a Series 600 was put was the modification of the co-pilot's instrument panel to represent a Sea Harrier FA2, in connection with the Blue Vixen radar trials, which began in September 1989. Blue Vixen was a nose-mounted radar, later fitted as standard to the Sea Harrier. A launch rail, complete with a dummy missile, was fitted under the starboard wing and the nose was extended to accommodate the trial radar system. The aircraft allocated for this work was ZF130, c/n 256059, and much of the work was carried out at Dunsfold. The work undertaken by this aircraft had been preceded by XW930 (c/n 25009), a Series 1 aircraft originally operated by the Civil Aviation Flying Unit.

The noise regulations introduced by the FAA in 1974 were now beginning to bite, and the 125 was the only aircraft in its class not operating with the new turbofan engines. It was a development that was unexpected but with consequences worldwide that changed the situation. In 1973, the Middle East oil producers, without warning and for no discernible reason, dramatically increased the price of oil. Within two years, the world market price of cents per barrel suddenly became dollars per barrel, followed by an inevitable recession in the business markets. The high hopes for the -600 were suddenly dashed and production rates were cut. Ultimately, only 72 of the type were built. The final aircraft in the series, c/n 256071, became G-BEES for a few months before being exported to the US.

Built as a -600A, this aircraft spent some time in North America before appearing on the Romanian register. It was later sold back to the US as N411GA. (Martin Chell)

This anonymous aircraft is actually G-AZHS, the second -600 development aircraft. It was first flown at Chester in 1971 and was later re-engined with the TFE731 to become the -700 prototype. (Gerry Manning)

Chapter 5
The -700

Rolls-Royce had pioneered the turbofan engine, and it was targeted largely towards the larger passenger aircraft. The advantages of a turbofan engine were understood even before the original design of the 125 was taking place. The turbojet, common on all aircraft at the time, compressed the air at a high velocity into a very hot chamber, whereas, by comparison, the turbofan operates in a much gentler way, by compressing the air into a larger and cooler chamber. This has the effect of making the cooler surrounding air blanket the noise from the core jet; the result is much higher engine efficiency. It also has the added benefit of reducing noise levels, thus eliminating the need for silencing baffles, reducing maintenance time and cost, as well as weight.

When the Viper became unsuitable because of the oil crisis of 1973–74, the Bristol Siddeley division of Rolls-Royce began work on a new derivation of the turbofan engine, designated the RB.401, specifically for business jets. The two principal engines were sub-divided into two types, -06 and -07, and ground testing did take place, even into the 1980s, but the Rolls-Royce bankruptcy meant there

A line-up of -700s at Chester for a publicity photo shows a typical range of colour schemes and operators. (David Powell collection)

This aircraft was supplied to the government of Zanzibar as a -700B in 1982. (Richard Vandervord)

Shell Aviation was the original owner of this aircraft before it went onto the Nigerian register. (Richard Vandervord)

The markings give a clue to the use of this aircraft. It was acquired from new in 1982 as a -700B for use by the Nigerian Federal Ministry Civil Aviation Flying Unit. (Gerry Manning)

Washington's National Airport is the backdrop for this photo as this Series 700A taxies. (Gerry Manning)

Originally the BAe -700 demonstrator for the US, this aircraft came to an unfortunate end when, as N720PT, it was written off on 28 May 2020 after landing illegally on an airstrip between the towns of Chunox and Sarteneja in northern Belize, close to the Mexican border, while on a drug-smuggling flight. (David Powell collection)

Originally delivered to Kuwait Airways in 1983, this -700B had an eventful life when it was stolen from Kuwait by Iraqi forces during an attack on Kuwait in 1990. It was flown to Baghdad and painted in Iraqi Airways colours (see below) and was found after the war. After being restored to Kuwait Airways, it passed through several owners and now flies on the Russian register. (Richard Vandervord)

9K-AGA was re-registered as YI-AKG by the Iraqis and found at a hideout near Saddam Hussein's palace after the war. (Photographer unknown)

Sister ship 9K-AGB was not so fortunate, however. Although it too was stolen from Kuwait, it was destroyed in a coalition attack on Baghdad Airport in February 1991. (Richard Vandervord)

Sadly, some of the 125's best attributes are now being put to use by drug-runners. Its ability to land almost anywhere and the ease of flying it have made it the aircraft of choice. This aircraft is shown as N818LD, the second time this registration had been used illegally. The aircraft is actually N925MC, c/n 257021. It is a 700A, found in northern Belize, near to the border with Mexico. An unsuccessful attempt had been made to burn the aircraft. (Belize Defence Force)

was a lack of funds for development. For a brief period, there was a collaborative venture with Pratt & Whitney Canada, but the project was eventually abandoned. In fact, Pratt & Whitney, following the Rolls-Royce decision, decided to develop an engine of its own. The jointly developed RB.401 engine would probably have been ideal for the 125, but a decision on a new engine had to be made before the engine had been finally tested.

Hawker Siddeley now had to look around the market for a new engine. The General Electric CF700 aft-fan engine had been the powerplant of choice for a 125 competitor, the Dassault 20. Like the Viper though, this engine was rapidly reaching the end of its useful life and was soon rejected. One company that seemed able to offer an alternative was the Garrett Company, part of AlliedSignal – a large US corporation specialising in control systems, avionics, turbochargers and aircraft engines. They were manufacturing an engine known as the TFE731, a geared turbofan, which had first been run in 1970 and introduced into service in 1972. The existence of gearing in a turbofan seemed unnecessary, and this initially dissuaded the design department from studying the engine further. However, further investigations revealed a number of significant improvements over similar engines. In a geared turbofan, between the fan and the low-pressure shaft, there is a reduction gearbox, which ultimately increases efficiency and reduces the weight of the powerplant. Some energy is lost as heat in the gearbox mechanism and the weight saved by not having the turbine and compressor stages fitted is partly offset by the gearbox. The gearbox, in fact, allowed flexibility in the engine, no matter what altitude it was operating at. It had been shown to use fuel at about half the average rate of the Viper, and this, together with a lower unit weight, would increase its potential range. In order to maintain the 125s centre of gravity, the engine would need to be fitted further aft than had been the case with the Viper. With the TFE731, both engines were built with the capability to drive both a hydraulic pump

Delivered new to the Irish Air Corps in 1980, this -700A was later exported to the US. (Richard Vandervord)

The appropriately registered G-OBAE, a 700A, is seen overhead Hatfield in a 1980 publicity shot. (David Powell collection)

This anonymous -700B, seen outside the factory at Chester, was soon to become G-MSFY. After spending some time on the Bermudan register, it now carries a Russian registration. (David Powell)

This -700B was delivered new to a Bahamian customer in 1979 and later became VP-CFI. See below. (Richard Vandervord)

The life of this -700B, formerly VP-CFI, ended unusually: it became part of a feature in front of the offices of luxury accommodation near Selby in North Yorkshire, UK. (Martin Chell)

Mozambique is just another country on the long list of those that applied the registration to the 125. This -700B, delivered in 1982, receives a full maintenance check. It is currently on the Russian register. (Martin Chell)

There's no secret about the ownership of this immaculate -700A, though it's unlikely it would ever be used for delivering pizza. (Gerry Manning)

An evening line-up of -700s outside the Chester factory. (David Powell collection)

Metrojet was the Hong-Kong-based owner of this -700B. (Gerry Manning)

This –700B was built in 1980 and was still flying in Russia 40 years later. (Gerry Manning)

Right: Dallah Avco took delivery of this Saudi Arabian-registered -700B, seen parked at Heathrow. (Richard Vandervord)

Below: Another Saudi-registered -700A, this time at Luton, UK. (Richard Vandervord)

Rolled out from Chester with pride during 1981 is -700 c/n 257172, the 700th 125 to be built. (David Powell)

Right: Seen here in the colours of Sibaviatrans, this Series 700B passed through several owners before becoming 6V-AIM, the fate of which is described in Chapter 10. (Martin Chell)

Below: General Electric of the US was the operator of this -700A when the photo was taken in 1996 while the aircraft was on approach to Heathrow, UK. (Gerry Manning)

Chapter 6

The -800

In April 1981, following the absorption of the various aircraft manufacturing entities into BAe, the parent company reaffirmed its intention to develop the 125 and various options, beginning with a completely new design, for which new wings and engines were being examined.

The -700 Series had sold well with, at one point, a new aircraft being ordered approximately every ten days. However, aircraft design can never stand still, not least because competitors are always looking for some innovation to improve their sales. It was time to consider improvements for the best-selling jet. The options being studied were an increase in fuselage length, plus increased engine thrust, using a more powerful version of the now successful TFE731. The possibility of a new wing was also under consideration.

The registration suffix of this -800 gives a clue to its owner, Union Pacific Railroad. It is seen here at Washington's National Airport. (Gerry Manning)

G-IFTF was originally G-GEIL, which itself was bought as a replacement for G-GAEL. See below. (Martin Chell)

G-GAEL, seen here at Miami, was involved in a wheels-up incident at Gander Airport, Canada, following which it was recovered by BAe and used for a time as a demonstrator. See Chapter 10. (Author's collection)

It was well-known that the 125 was a robust aircraft, but its robustness was dramatically demonstrated when, on 7 August 1988, the starboard engine was hit by a missile, resulting in the complete loss of the engine and considerable damage to the aircraft. The full story is in Chapter 10.

G-BUCR, an -800B, receives attention at the Chester service centre. (David Powell)

Seen here at a factory open day in 1983, this -800 was actually an 'A' Series aircraft. It was later re-registered as G-UWWB 'Up Where We Belong', which was a marketing phrase used by BAe at the time. (David Powell)

Unsurprisingly perhaps, the registration N800BA has been used no less than nine times, including once on a Cessna 414A. In this case, the aircraft is c/n 258001, the same aircraft as in the photo above, being rolled out during a publicity day at Chester. The aircraft in the background is the 748 demonstrator, which brought the journalists to Chester. (Author's collection)

Another demonstrator, this time the first to be designed by the Rover Car Company, which BAe bought in 1988. The striking exterior colour and design was also used earlier on G-BSUL. (David Powell)

Above left: The interior of G-RAAR, which received mixed reviews. (Author's collection)

Above right: An air-to-air publicity photo of an 800A. (David Powell collection)

A new aircraft build was quickly ruled out based on time and cost. Moreover, the -700 was selling well, so why start at the beginning again? Appropriate modifications to the -700 to reflect the developments taking place in the world of aircraft manufacturing would, the board believed, be sufficient to maintain the aircraft's competitive edge. The designers eventually settled upon an improved design for the wings, which would produce an improved aerofoil profile, enabling a slight increase in speed. This also incorporated a redesign of the wing leading edge, since new legislation had been brought in to reduce the possibility of bird-strike damage. A seemingly unimportant 3in (7.62cm) was added to the fuselage length, but, in fact, the benefits of this were considerable, since they were added to the flight deck. The workload for pilots flying an executive jet differs little from that of a commercial airliner. They are often flying in and out of major airports, subject to the same rules and regulations, but arguably the net worth of those in the cabin and the company they represent is significantly higher than those on a typical scheduled airline flight. With this in mind, the flight deck was enlarged, enabling the pilots to stretch their legs on longer journeys, and the panel of circuit breakers was moved to the rear wall of the flight deck, to make it more easily accessible. Another benefit for the pilots was the introduction of the 'glass cockpit,' known in the industry as the electronic flight instrument system (EFIS), featuring several TV-like screens rather than a bank of instruments.

Few of these changes were immediately obvious, but one major development, which was very apparent and well received, was that of the new style of windscreen. The spilt V-shaped windscreen of the previous series had been replaced by two large curved panels. However, the effect was not just cosmetic. Apart from eliminating the need for windscreen wipers, the new arrangement meant that, aerodynamically, it reduced drag – the aerodynamic force that opposes an aircraft's motion through the air – and also the noise level on the flight deck. The panels were made from specially designed acrylic, which had the additional benefit of repelling water droplets, hence the reason for discontinuing with the wipers. For a brief time, a rain-shedding air blower was installed on the captain's side, but it was soon deemed unnecessary and was discontinued on later models.

At the tail of the aircraft, other modifications were incorporated. The dorsal fuel tank, added to provide a little extra range, was removed, but to maintain the same level of fuel capacity, the ventral fuel tank was enlarged, which, like the improved windscreen design, had the effect of reducing drag. There was no lengthening of the cabin as such. BAe believed that, at that time, the cabin proportions were the optimum. In the world of business jets, aircraft types are often referred to in terms of cabin size: small, medium and large. From its earliest days, the 125 had always been classed as a mid-cabin aircraft and this could not be changed, but the opportunity was taken to redesign the cabin interior. The 'wide-bodies' – Boeing 747s, DC-10s and L1011s – were now being used on worldwide routes, and it was important to bring that look into the business jet. Thermal and acoustic insulation was maintained at the same level, while the choice of fabrics, galley equipment and passenger service units was greater than ever before. Overall, there were few criticisms of the 125, but one that was aired frequently was the lack of baggage space and later in its life the -800 interior was redesigned so the baggage could be carried in a pannier beneath the aircraft, thus freeing up more space in the cabin. At the forward end, the four individual seats could be rotated through 180° and a table folded into the centre of this arrangement to form a 'club' configuration, whereby the four seats would now face the table.

Last but by no means least, an upgraded version of the proven Garrett TFE-731 engine was now available. This was known as the -5 and apart from offering almost 10 per cent more power, was able to reduce fuel consumption. With all the innovations now incorporated, flight testing began in May 1983, using c/n 258001, G-BKTF, which had initially been registered as N800BA for publicity purposes but was, in fact, a Series 'A' aircraft. For trial purposes, much of which took place at Hatfield, it was equipped with an instrument probe on the nose, designed to measure airspeed more accurately; a static drogue was attached to the tail, and behind the tail cone was fitted a large package containing a stall recovery parachute. Once equipped, the aircraft carried out a very comprehensive series of performance evaluations. The second aircraft, c/n 258002, first flew on 24 June 1983. It was painted all white initially and carried the registration G-DCCC – the Roman numerals for 800. It was used for individual trials in Zimbabwe, the United Arab Emirates, and Morocco.

Shortly after this photo was taken, the registration was changed to P4-AMF. It is currently registered as YV2837. The aircraft is sometimes shown as having an 'A' suffix but, in fact, it is a 'B' model. (Gerry Manning)

Again, the suffix gives a clue to the owner. Ayrton Senna, the Formula One racing driver, bought this -800A in 1990. He liked the aircraft so much that he learnt to fly it. (Pedro Aragão)

Above: Originally produced as a C-29A and serialled 88-0271, this -800A was transferred to the US Federal Aviation Administration (FAA) in 1991 for flight inspection purposes. It is seen here at the rebuilt Basra Airport in Iraq, following the Gulf War. (David Hedges)

Left: HZ105 of the Saudi Arabian Air Force undergoes maintenance at Chester. The aircraft is an -800B. (Gerry Manning)

The third aircraft was more representative of what the -800 was to become. This was c/n 258003 and registered as G-BKUW, but unlike the previous two aircraft, it had now been fitted with the full EFIS suite. Unlike its predecessors, 'UW was fated to travel to the colder areas of the world, with cold weather trials in Canada, Greenland and Iceland. All three aircraft were built as 'A' Series aircraft and, in fact, 'UW was later registered as N800BA and flown to the US to be used as a demonstrator. The aircraft type received full certification in May 1984, and the first aircraft delivered, a Series 'B', was to Heron International in the UK as G-GAEL.

To celebrate the sale of the 500th 125, a 'fly-in' was arranged at Chester. The event took place on 29 October 1980. The 500th aircraft, a Series A, was sold, along with the preceding aircraft, to Manufacturers Hanover Corporation, a large banking institution based in New York, now part of J P Morgan. It was also the 300th aircraft to be sold in the US. By 14 July 1988, the total had reached 700. Despite a worldwide downturn in the economy, the -800 continued to sell well and on 24 October 1987, the 100th -800 was sold to Alcan of Montreal.

Interiors

One of the advantages of buying a new business jet is that, to a large degree, the customer can specify an interior of their choice. The limitations are only those of the airworthiness regulations in the country where the aircraft will be registered and the imagination of the customer; for example, in those days, none of the authorities would allow showers to be fitted, fearing the damage that would be caused if there was a leak, although a number of customers asked about this option. If the aircraft was company-owned, then the layout would typically be based on eight seats, with a small galley to provide hot drinks and snacks. Some company-owned aircraft had as many as 12 seats in them in cases where they were used basically as a communications aircraft between sites. In almost every case, all the available space in the aircraft was put to effective use.

Where private customers where involved, the interior could be any combination of seats and other interior fittings, and any combination of colours. The Middle Eastern customers tended to prefer large seats, lots of gold trimmings and thick carpets, for example. European customers often asked for wood veneer trim, but however bizarre the request, the interior design team could usually work out a satisfactory solution. Since the launch of the -800, their job had been made easier by the wider availability of materials; new types of fabrics and fittings were now available, which could be adapted to produce a more sophisticated finish. The job of accurately designing the interior was made easier by the emergence of computer-aided design. Previously, the suggestions would be sketched out on boards, but with the best will in the world, they did not give a totally accurate impression. When BAe took over the Rover Car Company in 1988, it invited the Rover design team to produce an interior for the 125-800 in the belief there might be a crossover between the two applications. However, following customer reaction to one of the designs, which was incorporated into a demonstrator aircraft, it became apparent that the original ideas were not well received. A second opportunity was offered to design the -1000, where the first three aircraft to come off the line were finished successfully by Rover.

The smallest space on the aircraft was reserved for the toilet, and there was little that could be done to give the impression of space. One idea that was tried out was to put a picture of a landscape on the wall. This was appreciated by some customers, but on one occasion the wife of a prospective customer went to use the toilet during a demonstration flight. As she opened the door, she screamed, closed the door and ran back into the cabin. It so happened that the mural chosen for the toilet was an aerial view of Mont Blanc, which was precisely where the aircraft was flying at the time and the lady concerned thought, at first glance, that a large piece of the tail had fallen off.

This aircraft came out of the factory as an -800B and was subsequently registered G-BSUL and used as a demonstrator. Despite being a 'B' Series aircraft, it was sold to the US. Sadly, it crashed at Owatonna Airport, Minnesota, on 31 July 2008, killing all on board. (Gerry Manning).

At the time this photo was taken in Sacramento, California, the -800A was owned by food producer H J Heinz. (Gerry Manning)

Left: This -800A, seen here in 2005 at Zürich, was bought as pre-owned in April 2004, before being sold on to the US in 2016. (Gerry Manning)

Below: One of the very few business jets on the Bangladesh register, S2-AHS was originally built as an -800A and sold in the US in 1982. It is being towed at Don Muang Airport in Bangkok in 2020. Note the addition of winglets. (Gerry Manning)

Chapter 7
The -1000

The success of the -800 had brought with it requests from existing and potential users for a larger aircraft with longer range. This had been thought about for some time, not least because the business jet market could offer a small cabin and short range, a medium cabin and medium range or a large cabin and long range, but not a combination of medium cabin and long range. It was not just the North American customers who were looking for longer range. Customers in the Pacific Rim countries had asked about a longer-range version too.

For a while, BAe had looked at stretching the -800, informally known as the -800 I (for improved). This was unrelated to the -800, which went into production as a medium cabin, medium-range aircraft. The -800 I was to be significantly larger than the -800 and would be powered by the ill-fated Rolls-Royce RB 401 engine. The planned range was approximately 3,500miles (5,600km), sufficient to fly from London to New York non-stop at airliner cruising speeds. Pratt & Whitney had taken out a production franchise on the RB 401, partly to circumvent potential US antitrust legislation, but it was not to be. The cancellation of the RB 401 also had a significant effect on BAe's thinking. An innovative design had been under consideration, where the parameters would have added fuel capacity, plus the TFE731-5BR engines. The problem here was that airframe design invariably runs ahead of engine design, and there was little that Garrett AiResearch could do in the short term to provide a more powerful version of the TFE731. This took the designers to Montreal, where Pratt & Whitney Canada was able to offer the PW305. This was actually part of a family of engines aimed at the business jet market, and variants of the engine had been selected for the Dassault 2000, the Cessna Citation and Latitude and the Gulfstream 200, all aircraft of a similar size to the proposed new aircraft, plus the engine came with a significant pedigree. Now, BAe could focus its efforts on achieving a larger range with a larger aircraft.

The series number was set at -1000 rather than 900. This intrigued many potential buyers, and especially the media, and many wondered if the jump had been made to avoid any confusion with the Dassault Falcon 900. The official line from BAe was that because it was not an upgrading of the -800, rather the product of new developments, it should not be confused with its predecessors. It is fair to say that, in addition to the

A development version of a -1000, still in zinc chromate and fitted with a probe, sits outside the Chester factory. (David Powell collection)

ADAC is Europe's largest motoring organisation, but this -1000A is equipped as an air ambulance for repatriation flights. (Martin Chell)

G-LRBJ (Long-Range Business Jet) was the fourth -1000 to be built and was used as a demonstrator. (Gerry Manning)

There was some confusion over the registration after this -1000B was delivered to the Turkmenistan government. It was delivered on a British registration because ICAO (International Civil Aviation Organization) had not yet issued a prefix for Turkmenistan registrations. Initially, they were given 'EK-', but then it was realised that the prefix had already been issued to Armenia and it was amended to 'EZ-'. (Author)

G-BUIX was a 1000A, used for a short period as a demonstrator. It is pictured here at Elista in southern Russia. (Author)

Right: Another shot of G-LRBJ, operating near Table Mountain in Cape Town. (David Powell collection)

Below: San Marino is another country in which it is now popular to register business jets. Here, the registration is applied to a BAe 1000B. (Martin Chell)

change of powerplant, many innovations were incorporated into the -1000. These included the fitting of full authority digital electronic control (FADEC). This allows the pilot to set the throttles to the correct position for a particular situation, at which point the FADEC takes over. There are those who believe that less fuel is used with this system. A new environmental control system was also installed. EFIS was now available and based on the experience with the -800, the Honeywell flight management system was chosen. It was not just about FADEC and EFIS either. Although more powerful than the TFE731, the specific fuel consumption in high-speed cruise with the PW305 proved to be lower, and there was an additional benefit in that the engines could be fitted with thrust reversers – the first time these had been fitted to the 125.

Having selected a new engine, the next challenge for the design team was to set about lengthening the fuselage. This is normally done by what is known in the business as 'plugs', i.e., additional sections of fuselage positioned before and/or after the wings. In this case, the complete fuselage was redesigned. The concern centred around the potential damage to the rear pressure bulkhead, which could be caused by engine debris. The -800 had not been able to meet this requirement and as a result, its ceiling is limited to 41,000ft (12,500m). The Hawker-designed 1000 had a secondary pressure bulkhead fitted, thus allowing a higher cruising altitude of 43,000ft (13,100m).

The -1000 was now 33in (83cm) longer than the -800, with 28in (71cm) being devoted to extending the cabin, which now included an additional window, and 5in (12cm) being added to the baggage area. The wing-body fairing was also improved, allowing a further 135 gal (614 lit) of fuel to be stored. The overall MTOW of the aircraft – 31,000lb (14,061kg) against the 27,400lb (12,428kg) of the -800 – meant that additional strengthening of the undercarriage was required. As ever with a new design, a considerable amount of test flying was required and this identified a number of irritating problems, mostly of an aerodynamic nature, but these were eventually solved. Another factor to be taken into account during the design process was the introduction of competitor aircraft, such as the Learjet 54/55 and Cessna Citation III.

With the introduction of the 1000, the dimensions of the 125 had changed considerably from the days of the prototypes, which had started its life as 43ft 6in (12.26m) long, with a wingspan of 44ft (13.41m). The later Hawker 1000 came out at 53ft 11in (16.45m), with a wingspan of 51ft 5in (15.7m), with the MTOW growing from 19,000lb (8,618kg) to 31,000lb (14,061kg). The first flight of the aircraft took place on 16 June 1990.

Below left: Once again, the clue to the owner is in the registration. Olayan Finance Corporation was the first owner of this Saudi Arabian-registered 1000B. (Gerry Manning)

Below right: The interior of the first -1000 demonstrator. (BAE Systems)

Chapter 8
The Variants

The versatility of the 125 design became more apparent as operators began to ask whether it was possible to fit the aircraft with specialised equipment. In 1986, the Swiss ambulance organisation, after a comprehensive evaluation, asked whether the aircraft could be fitted out to perform the duties of a flying intensive-care unit. They ordered two -800 Series, which were fitted with a vast array of medical equipment. This gave the aircraft the capability to load two stretchers, a full leg-rest chair and seats for a doctor and nurse. The aircraft were also fitted with inertial navigation systems – an innovation at the time – allowing the aircraft to operate independently of the usual ground-based systems.

The 125 was also chosen for the flight inspection role. This requires the installation of a considerable amount of equipment in order to verify the accuracy of the various navigational aids available to pilots. One such customer was the US Air Force (USAF). It had previously used the T-39 (known as the

Right: A Raytheon-built U-125A of the Japanese Air Self-Defense Force (JASDF) seen here at Hayakuri Air Force Base, Japan. (Gerry Manning)

Below: A second example of a Raytheon-built U-125A, seen here at Nagoya. (Gerry Manning)

Above: **An error was made when applying the serial number to this C-29A. It reads as 80270. In fact, that serial belongs to an A-10, and it should read as 88-0270. Since it is a new aircraft and it was present at the Farnborough Airshow in 1990, the fiscal year of purchase would have been 1988. (Gerry Manning)**

Left: **A Chester-built navigation inspection aircraft, designated U-125 by the JASDF. (Gerry Manning)**

Sabreliner in civil use), and the C-140 (The Lockheed JetStar) for this purpose. Six aircraft were ordered, initially under the designation C-FIN (combat flight inspection and navigation) but redesignated as the C-29A in service. The aircraft entered service at the headquarters of Air Mobility Command, Scott Air Force Base in Illinois, and in 1991, during the Gulf War, the aircraft were used to inspect facilities in the coalition-friendly countries of the Middle East. However, later in 1991, it was decided to place the aircraft under the control of the FAA. A new base was set up at Oklahoma City, with two aircraft detached to Hawaii and two to Tokyo. The remaining two aircraft were based at the Rhein-Main Air Base near Frankfurt. However, this operation was to prove costly and inefficient, so the aircraft were returned to Oklahoma. They were repainted and re-registered as civil aircraft and are now operated and maintained under the auspices of the FAA, although the aircraft are flown by both USAF and civilian crews.

Success breeds success, and it was not long before representatives from the Japanese Air Self-Defense Force (JASDF) visited Chester. They were running a programme known as FC-X, for which they required an aircraft to perform similar duties to the C-29A. This would mark the first time since the end of World War Two that the Japanese forces would seriously consider a non-American aircraft. An order for three aircraft was placed and these were later designated as U-125; the first aircraft was handed over on 16 December 1992. Additional aircraft were ordered subsequently, designated U-125A and used for search and rescue missions.

Right: A batch of three U-125s being prepared for the JASDF at the Chester factory. (David Powell collection)

Below: Wearing its class 'B' registration and here in its zinc chromate primer, this basic -800 would be flown to the US in this condition to be fitted out for work as a U-125A (search and rescue aircraft) for the JASDF. It later became 73-2005. (Gerry Manning)

The 125 and drug-running

One role of the 125 that could never have been foreseen, and is certainly unwanted, is that of a drug-runner. The use of the 125 in drug-running has become increasingly prevalent in recent years, and while this particular variant is anything but official, the incidences of its use are such that the whole practice is deserving of further description. Not least because, for its purpose, the cabin is stripped out to the extent that the interior resembles that of a regular cargo-carrying aircraft – the seats, galley and even the toilet are removed. This is done to reduce weight, as well as to increase the cargo-carrying capacity of the aircraft.

In the early days of drug-running, particularly in the case of cocaine, the product was typically moved by land or sea to the US border. This was done in relatively small quantities, just tens of kilos. However, the exponential growth in demand meant that new ways of moving it had to be found. The only obvious aviation involvement in incidents of drug-running during the late 1970s and early

1980s was the use of DC-3s, with the large freight doors actually removed, to take drums of petrol from the larger cities to the remote towns and villages in Colombia where the cocaine was produced. The doors were taken off to provide adequate ventilation during the flight (petrol is used to break down the cocaine leaves into powder). As the demand for the drug increased so did the attempts to at least curtail the illicit trade and the traffickers had to come up with new ideas.

It is no secret that business jets are generally subjected to fewer security checks than other aircraft, and since the drug barons were obviously users of such aircraft, they quickly became aware of this. It then became apparent to them that here was a method by which larger quantities of drugs, which would be less subject to potential scrutiny, could be moved more easily. The sales brochures for the 125 described it as rugged and able to land on unprepared runways. They also made much of its reliability and the fact that it was easy to fly. While these were all excellent selling points, they were also the precise qualities that made it the aircraft of choice for the drug trade. Initially, the drugs were moved directly from small strips, often a forest clearing in the lowlands of Colombia, to Mexico for onward transmission by road into the US. However, once it was realised that this route was being used, the authorities began to monitor the traffic more strictly and the flights were switched to the Bahamas, where Colombian Carlos Lehder who, in effect, was the logistics manager for the Medellín Cartel, bought an island in the Bahamas known as Norman's Cay, which, between 1978 and 1982, became notorious as a drug-smuggling hub. Those who already lived on the island were 'encouraged to leave', either by threat or force. Lehder arranged for the island's runway to be lengthened to 3,300ft (1,000m), so that aircraft up to the size of a DC-3 or C-46 could land there. To protect the island, he had radar fitted and full-time guards with dogs carried out patrols. The cocaine would be flown in from Colombia and then reloaded onto smaller aircraft for the short flight into the southern states of the US, such as Florida, Georgia and the Carolinas.

Following Lehder's arrest in 1987, new methods had to be found for transporting the drugs. The small twin-engined aircraft, such as Piper Aztecs, which had handled the traffic previously, were no longer large or fast enough to fulfil the market demand for the drugs or reliably carry it for any significant distance. At the same time, the authorities, aware of the increasing volume of traffic, began to install additional radar coverage to capture aircraft flying at low level.

The 125 had sold well in Mexico; more than 100 aircraft have appeared on the register, many through the used aircraft market from the US, as their owners traded up to the -800 or another type. Additionally, there are many US-registered aircraft freely operating there. Today, an older used -700 can sell for less than US$400,000, with a similarly used -800 typically costing US$500,000. With the price of cocaine currently hovering around the US$30,000 per kilo mark, the mathematical equation is simple and the 125 quickly becomes the aircraft of choice for the drug-runners.

Perhaps the most notorious aspect of this was the use of the registration N818LD. This registration has been used on no less than three different aircraft. It was in 2018 that the first evidence of a 125 being used in drug-running operations became known. On 3 April that year, a -700A Series aircraft was found abandoned at a temporary airstrip in Aguaro-Guariquito, a designated Venezuelan national park located about 200 miles (320km) south of the capital, Caracas. It was covered by tree branches and wearing a taped-on registration, N818LD, which would later be used several times. In fact, the aircraft was XB-PDD, built as c/n 257129 which, since leaving the Chester factory in 1981, had worn ten different registrations but had only carried the Mexican registration for two months before being found there. The second aircraft to carry the registration was N926MC, a Series -700A, c/n 257021, built in 1978. The aircraft had carried seven previous legitimate registrations, with the current owner being shown as a trusteeship based in Albuquerque, New Mexico. This one was found abandoned on a road that runs between the small towns of San Estevan and Progresso in Belize on 24 April 2018. Scorch marks on the wings suggested that unsuccessful attempts had been made to

Above: Another country that uses the 125 for flight inspections is Brazil. This is a long-standing relationship that goes back to the delivery of the first Series 3 in 1968. (Helio Bastos Salmon)

Right: An unidentified 125 on a drug-smuggling run is found on a road in a remote part of Mexico. In most of these cases, the goods have been removed and there is no sign of the crew.

set the aircraft on fire. Undeterred by this, the Belize Defence Force later flew the aircraft to its base in Ladyville. The aircraft was cancelled from the US register on 30 December 2019. On 26 January 2020, the third aircraft to carry this registration was found in San Andrés, another nature reserve in the El Petén region of Guatemala. This aircraft had been built as a Series 'B' in 1984 with c/n 258013 and supplied to a British owner. It was later exported to the US, where it was converted to a Series 'A' and carried several other registrations. The correct registration was N305AG, shown as being owned by Aircraft Guaranty Corporation, based in Onalaska, Texas. This aircraft was later flown to the Guatemalan Air Force Northern Air Command base at Mundo Maya Airport. A video showing the dramatic departure of the aircraft from the jungle strip where it was found has been posted on the internet. It is believed the aircraft has now been taken on charge by the Guatemalan Air Force and re-registered as 2020. Its US registration was finally cancelled on 20 May 2021 as 'exported to Mexico'.

The registration N818LD does exist. It belongs to a -700A Series aircraft, c/n 257192, built in 1982. It appears to have led an innocuous life having, at one point, been owned by the Monsanto Company (formerly Monsanto Chemicals). The aircraft was posted as 'withdrawn from use' in St. Petersburg, Florida, on 6 June 2017 and then cancelled from the US register on 3 October 2020. However, somewhat surprisingly, it was then restored to the register on 20 May 2021, with the owner shown as Aviation Trust Company, Oklahoma.

Currently, no less than 40 125s have been involved in suspected drug-running operations.

Chapter 9
The Takeovers

On 1 May 1992, the board of BAe took the decision to remove their name from the 125 division, renaming it Corporate Jets Ltd, and invitations were solicited for either a majority-ownership buyer or a complete takeover. However, later that year, at the September NBAA convention in Dallas, the company announced it was withdrawing from the sale. The reason for this was not a change of mind as such; it was more to do with the fact that BAe was moving Corporate Jets into a subsidiary of British Aerospace Inc. and relocating the headquarters from Hatfield to Little Rock, Arkansas. BAe then took the decision to sell the Corporate Jets Division to Raytheon, the US multinational aerospace and defence corporation, perhaps best known as the manufacturer of the Patriot missile. The deal, renaming the company Raytheon Corporate Jets (RCJ), was completed on 1 June 1993. The headquarters of RCJ were to be in Little Rock, Arkansas.

For a while, production of the 125 continued at Chester, but the ultimate aim was to produce the aircraft from scratch in the US, and as the assembly plants in the US became familiar with the building techniques of the aircraft, the work transferred across the Atlantic. From 1996 onwards, the assembled sections and components of the aircraft were shipped to Wichita, Kansas, for final assembly.

The last 125 to be built at Chester, a Series 'A' aircraft, was rolled out on 22 April 1997. It was c/n 258337, a -800 and first flown on a 'B' registration as G-5-868 on 29 April 1997. It was registered in the US as N337XP. The first aircraft to be completely assembled in the US was c/n 258297. The fuselage and wing assemblies had been taken by road from Chester to Stansted, from where they were flown to Wichita on 7 October 1995. With Raytheon as the owner, the first registration it carried was

An unusual visitor to the Chester service centre was this Kazakh-registered Hawker 900XP, UP-HA001. Initially, ICAO gave Kazakhstan the 'UN-' prefix, but to avoid confusion with aircraft operating for the United Nations, it was changed to 'UP-'. (Martin Chell)

Also at the Chester service centre is D-COLD a Hawker 800XP. (Martin Chell)

Another Hawker 800XP, this time arriving at Manchester. (Gerry Manning)

Guernsey, one of the British Channel Islands, has become a popular place to register business jets. This Hawker 750 is a typical example. (Martin Chell)

M-XJET, an 800XP, is registered in another British island – the Isle of Man which, in recent times, has been allocated its own 'M-' prefix. (Martin Chell)

Left: This Israeli-registered Hawker 800XP is parked in rather gloomier conditions than it normally experiences. (Martin Chell)

Below: Another 800XP, this time Hungarian-registered, outside the Chester service centre. (Martin Chell)

Above: This Hawker 850XP was supplied new to this Irish operator. (Gerry Manning)

Right: N535RV, a Hawker 800XP, passes some ongoing construction work at Manchester Airport. (Gerry Manning)

N297XP, but it was later sold on as the Hawker 800XP. Despite the upheavals, the 1,000th aircraft of the 125 family was delivered in April 1998. The fact that 1,000 aircraft had been built with the same jigs and tooling stands was testament not only to the original design but also to the continuous design improvements that continued to make the aircraft attractive in the marketplace.

In early 2002, at the National Business Aviation Convention in New Orleans, Raytheon announced that the Hawker and Beechcraft brands would make a combined return to the world of business aviation, following the events of 9/11. By 2006, Raytheon had decided to concentrate on its core defence business and put the aircraft manufacturing business up for sale. There were a number of suitors, including the Carlyle Group and Cerberus Capital Management, but the bid was won by Onex Partners and Goldman Sachs Capital Partners operating under the name of Hawker Beechcraft Corporation (HBC) from March 2007. HBC opened a new manufacturing facility in Chihuahua, Mexico, soon afterwards and concluded an agreement with Hawker Pacific of Singapore to become an authorised service centre.

The connection, though, was that Raytheon had bought the Beech Aircraft Corporation as long ago as 1980, and Beech Aircraft had previously been involved in a partnership with the 125, but despite the continuing success of the type, Raytheon sold the product on to this new company, now named as Hawker Beechcraft. It continued to use the brand name Hawker, although in some circles the aircraft was still referred to as the Raytheon 125. Raytheon, however, insisted upon using the name Hawker to acknowledge the Hawker Siddeley lineage. To establish a new image for the 125, the two models were quickly renamed as the Hawker 800 and Hawker 1000. The choice was fortuitous because it had long been used to describe the aircraft in North America and Australia, and in other countries too. The marketing effort was now more focused on North America and, by extension, Mexico.

Between 2006 and 2013, the 125 Series were built by HBC. The economic crisis of 2008 was soon upon HBC, however, and the company began to find it increasingly difficult to service its debts. The problems had begun with the worldwide financial recession of 2008; the company began to lay off significant numbers of the workforce and by August 2009 more than 3,000 employees – a figure representing 25 per cent of its workforce – had been laid off, with the company saying that one of the biggest slowdowns had been in the fractional ownership of business jets, adding that these would not necessarily be the last of the cutbacks. NetJets had cancelled orders for 12 aircraft and deferred other deliveries for a further two years. By the end of 2009, further layoffs had taken place, leaving the workforce reduced by about 36 per cent. The unions were now becoming increasingly concerned about events and asked HBC for an explanation, but the prospects were gloomy.

The company replied that it had lost more than US$63m in the first quarter of 2010 alone, even though there had been additional job cuts in 2009. Management announced that thought had been given to moving the work to Louisiana or Mississippi, where labour rates were traditionally lower, or possibly even outside the US. Further discussions with the unions took place, and they recommended that their members accept the 10 per cent pay cut and higher insurance contributions that HBC had offered, in order to forestall this. However, the majority voted against the deal, believing that HBC were about to leave Wichita anyway. Finally, in December 2010, the Kansas state government stepped in with a US$40m incentive package.

All this was to no avail, however, because by September 2011, the company was saddled with US$2.14bn of outstanding debt, and by March 2012 the company had agreed a deal for US$120m

Bought new from the manufacturer, this Estonian-registered 750XP sports a smart colour scheme. (Martin Chell)

Winglets began to be fitted to the 800XPs. The Viking emblem gives a clue to the aircraft's Danish registration. (Martin Chell)

of interim financing to recapitalise the company and persuaded lenders to defer repayments of the outstanding interest until late June 2012. Further interest payments went into default and speculation began to appear in the media that the company was in serious financial difficulties.

An offer to buy the company was made by Superior Aviation of Beijing, a private company that had previously purchased the rights to manufacture Brantly helicopters under licence and was making progress in developing remotely piloted aerial vehicles. Failures in the negotiations were believed to be the result of cultural differences, and by 18 October of that year, the potential deal had fallen through and production of the 125 was discontinued. The company ultimately recovered from bankruptcy and was relaunched under the previous Beechcraft name. However, it had been decided that no further jet-powered aircraft would be built, and all production of the 125 ceased completely.

By April 2012, HBC had defaulted on its interest payments to such a degree that on 3 May 2012, the company filed under Chapter 11 of the US bankruptcy code – the system by which a company in financial difficulties is given permission to stay in business for a limited period – in order for a reorganisation plan to be put in place to deal with its debt.

Production of the 125 had come to standstill. With nowhere else to turn, the company decided to discontinue business jet production as part of the restructuring and was finally released from bankruptcy in February 2013, calling itself simply Beechcraft Corporation. Along with the decision to no longer produce jet-powered aircraft, the name of Hawker Beechcraft would cease to exist.

The decision by Hawker Beechcraft in May 2013 to offer its jet division for sale brought a swift halt to production, with just 73 aircraft being built. As a consequence, there was a lack of confidence in the aircraft by potential buyers. This was exacerbated by the many deficiencies that the aircraft carried. Upgrades were offered by the manufacturer, but often had to be made to order by Textron Aviation. One operator of 16 aircraft admitted that, at one point, the fleet was down to three dispatchable aircraft because it was awaiting parts. By 2018, the early production aircraft were being offered for US$4m, little more than the engines' value as scrap, partly due to the fact that operators were buying early used models simply for their parts.

Pilatus of Switzerland, perhaps sensing that all was not well at HBC, had seen a potential a gap in the mid-size business jet market and began to design its own business jet version in 2007. Bearing an uncanny resemblance to the 125-800, the first aircraft was rolled out on 1 August 2014, and the first customer delivery took place in February 2018. By January 2021, the 100th aircraft had been delivered and, at the time of writing, the Pilatus order book continues to fill.

With more than 1,600 based on the original design having been built over a period of more than 50 years, the 125, which in its various forms had been operated by heads of state, the military of more than a dozen nations and more than 50 well-known companies, was no longer in production. Its ghost lives on though, in the Pilatus PC-24.

The Hawker Series

750

Sometimes described as the '800 Lite'. The first flight of this derivative took place on 23 August 2007, and certification was awarded in February 2008. It differed from the 800 in that the ventral fuel tank was replaced by an externally accessed baggage pannier, a modification frequently requested by potential customers. However, this has the effect of slightly reducing the range. It was introduced to compete with the Citation XLS and the Learjet 60. Just 48 of the type were built, with production ending in 2012.

Another aircraft bought new from the manufacturer in 1998 is this 800XP. Since then, it has been on the registers of the US, Britain, the Isle of Man, and is currently on the Indian register as VT-VAP. (Martin Chell)

Originally supplied to Harley Davidson, this 800XP was bought by Tamir Airways in 2018. (Martin Chell)

850XP

This version was certified for operation in March 2006 and is distinguished from the 800XP by the fact that winglets are fitted, giving it a slight increase in range. Thrust reversers were standard equipment on this model, along with an improved brake system, allowing it to operate off runways shorter than those of the standard 800. It had a redesigned interior and upgraded avionics and was introduced to fill the gap left by the 1000 model when its production was terminated. Production of the 850XP ended in 2009 after 100 aircraft had been built.

900XP

This model was developed directly from the 850XP and first became available in 2007. It was fitted with Honeywell TFE731-50BR powerplants to offer increased range. Other benefits over the 850XP included better fuel efficiency, aerodynamics and performance ability, all of which were assisted by the fitting of updated winglets. The combination of these gave the aircraft an excellent performance from hot and high airfields. The 900XP variant was introduced in 2006, but production ended just six years later, following the bankruptcy of Hawker Beechcraft. A total of 183 aircraft were produced.

Hawker 800 N84BA (Bell Atlantic) is parked at Washington National in this photo. (Gerry Manning)

The use of number prefixes, as seen on this 800XP, allows all sorts of interesting registrations to be created... (Martin Chell)

1000

Production was carried over from the standard aircraft built at Chester, but all aircraft were built in the 'A' range and designed to fly coast-to-coast within the US. A typical cabin arrangement would feature eight seats and a galley. With a price tag more than $3m higher than the 800XP, the type was never a big seller, and production ceased in 1997 after just six years, following the delivery of the 52nd aircraft.

4000

In November 1996, Raytheon had launched a newer version of the Series 1000, to be known initially as the Hawker Horizon, and later as the Hawker 4000. First flights of the aircraft were due to take place in 1999, with certification and initial customer deliveries due expected in 2001. This was the largest aircraft Raytheon had ever built. It was to be marketed as being in the 'super mid-size' category. The wings were manufactured by Fuji Heavy Industries in Japan and then transported to Raytheon's manufacturing facility in Wichita for assembly. Carbon composites were to be used for the first time in the construction of the aircraft.

Manufacturing was delayed, and the first flight did not take place until 11 August 2001. The second and third prototypes made their maiden flights on 10 May and 31 July 2002. That year, a development aircraft was exhibited at the NBAA convention in Orlando, Florida. Given the events of the previous year, this was a somewhat muted occasion. The aircraft came with a guaranteed minimum of 3,100nm (5,741km), with an expectation of certification being completed by late 2003 and deliveries to commence in early 2004. In December 2005, NetJets had placed an order for 50 aircraft, the largest order the company had ever received, with its European division also placing an order for 32 aircraft, for delivery between 2008 and 2016. By March 2007, there were more than 150 orders for the type. On 21 November 2006, it was announced that the aircraft had received its Federal Aviation Regulation Part 25 certification. Further orders followed, including one from BJETS for ten aircraft, but by the time the original customers began to take their deliveries, there were a number of strong competitors in the marketplace, including the Cessna Citation X, the Dassault Falcon 2000 and the Embraer Legacy 600.

Hawker 850XP HS-CPG seen here on finals for Phuket, Thailand, in February 2017. (Gerry Manning)

Chapter 10
Individual Histories

It should be no surprise that in a build of more than 1,000 aircraft, there would be a number of unusual events in which the aircraft became involved. Set out below, there follows a number of descriptions concerning some of the more bizarre incidents that occurred. They are arranged in c/n order.

25005 G-ASNU Series 1, Air Hanson

The 125 is probably the only business jet ever to have been hijacked. On 30 June 1967, the aircraft was chartered by Moïse Tshombe, who at the time had been the Prime Minister of Katanga and Congo, for a flight between the Spanish Mediterranean islands of Ibiza and Mallorca. Tshombe was the President of Katanga, a mineral-rich southeasterly province of what was then known as Zaire – previously the Belgian Congo. Shortly after its independence from Belgium, there was a feud between Tshombe and the President of Zaire, now known as the Democratic Republic of the Congo. Despite United Nations (UN) intervention, Katanga became part of Zaire. In 1965, Tshombe fled to Spain and was given asylum.

After taking off from Ibiza, the aircraft, with nine people on board, was hijacked at gunpoint by a member of the French secret service and forced to fly to Algeria. The aircraft landed at the major Algerian Air Force base at Boufarik, 19 miles (30km) southwest of Algiers. Upon landing, Tshombe and his companions were arrested, as were the British pilots. A request by the UN to immediately release the pilots and the aircraft was refused by the Algerians. Then, after a number of representations, the British government sent a diplomatic note to Algeria suggesting that if the releases did not take place forthwith, it would consider the hijacking an act of hostility towards the UK. The pilots were released on 22 September 1967 and returned to the UK with a fanfare of publicity. The aircraft was finally returned on 18 April 1968, and the crew returned to flying.

Tshombe died in captivity on 29 June 1969.

25007 F-BKMF Series 1, Air Affaires

On 5 June 1966, this aircraft was taking part in an air display at Nice Côte d'Azur Airport. It had taken off from Cannes a little earlier, and the plan was for it to make three flypast manoeuvres down the runway at Nice. The first pass was at a low height directly over the runway; the crew then made a second pass in the opposite direction. While making a right-hand turn to reach an altitude of 2,000ft (610m), the aircraft appeared to stall and immediately crashed into the Mediterranean Sea.

It is believed the crash was caused by the wing design limits being exceeded, while the crew were trying to avoid a stall. This, in turn, ruptured the fuel tank and the aircraft, being at a relatively low level, could not be recovered from this manoeuvre.

25096 N235KC Series 1A, Kellogg Company

The aircraft was taken illegally from Miami International Airport on the evening of 22 November 1966. No flight plan was filed, and there was only one pilot on board. There was also one passenger, his spouse. The aircraft took off without permission from Air Traffic Control (ATC), headed for Freeport in the Bahamas. However, during the approach to Freeport, the aircraft descended below minima and struck the surface of the water, crashing into the sea about 4.5 miles (7.2km) short of the runway at Pinder Point. The pilot, aged 33, who had 6,300 hours on his licence, of which 152 were on type, and was instrument rated, survived with serious injuries, but the body of his spouse was never recovered. The aircraft was less than six months old. The aircraft is also shown as belonging to Florida Commuter Airlines. Little else is known about the incident.

25099 5N-AER Series 1B, Nigerian Air Force

This aircraft appears to have been fated from the beginning of its life. It was originally supplied as HB-VAU to TransAir Suisse, which appear to have been an intermediary in the transaction, on 26 October 1966. It was then re-registered as 5N-AER the following month, with the owner being shown as the Biafra Air Force. The aircraft was flown first to Lagos and then seized following a delivery flight to Enugu, which, at the time, was the capital of Biafra, a breakaway province within Nigeria. After some negotiation, the aircraft was returned to the UK, where it was taken care of by the McAlpine service centre at Luton. It was returned to Nigeria again in September 1967 where, when parked at Port Harcourt, it was attacked by rocket fire just a few days after arriving. It was next seen stored in February 1968 in São Tomé and Príncipe, an island nation in the Gulf of Guinea. On 10 September 1969, it was re-registered as N2246 to a company called North American Aircraft Trading Inc. (NAAT), a company founded by Hank Wharton, who had been instrumental in organising the Biafran Airlift, a humanitarian relief operation that transported food and medicine to Biafra during its secession from Nigeria between 1967 and 1970.

It was then re-registered on 19 October 1973 as N121AC to a Mr Ronald L Hauck of Naranja, Florida, while still stored in São Tomé. Just 14 days later, there was an ownership change back to NAAT, but the aircraft remained stored. Attempts were made to repair the aircraft and fly it to the US, but they appear to have been unsuccessful, possibly because there was some doubt about the accuracy of the information in the logbooks. Finally, the aircraft was returned to Nigeria in 1975 and used as an instructional airframe by the Nigerian Air Force technical school in Zaria, central Nigeria. The whole story was the subject of a TV documentary some years ago.

25120 G-AVGW Series 3B, Beecham Pharmaceutical Group

The aircraft was operated by Autair International on behalf of Beecham. On 23 December 1967, it was operating a training flight for the first officer to complete his conversion training to the type. A number of flights were made locally and the plan was to finish the training detail with a simulated engine failure on take-off, followed by an asymmetric approach and single-engined landing. At the time of take-off, the engine failure was simulated, but for reasons unknown the aircraft climbed to just 300ft (91m), before descending rapidly and crashing onto the roof of the nearby Vauxhall Motors car factory about 800 yards (731m) to the west of Runway 26, as it was designated at the time. A large fire ensued and both pilots were killed. Fortunately, at the time of the accident, the factory was closed for the Christmas holidays, otherwise the death toll would have been significantly higher.

25175 Series 400A G-AWPC/N217F/YV-825CP/N272B/N773AA/XB-MGM

This aircraft was originally fitted with the Viper engine and later converted to a -400. On 4 November 2013, the aircraft left Querétaro Airport in central Mexico and made an intermediate stop, presumably for refuelling, at Bonaire in the Dutch Caribbean, following which it filed a flight plan for La Ceiba, a town on the northern coast of Honduras. However, the aircraft was intercepted after entering

Venezuelan airspace and followed for about 40 minutes, before being forced by the Venezuelan Air Force to land on a remote airstrip 8 miles (13km) north of the town of Buena Vista in the state of Apure. This is an area that borders Colombia and is known for cross-border smuggling. From there, the aircraft would fly to Central America, where the drug is moved on by Mexican cartels to the US. The occupants of the aircraft immediately fled the scene, but the authorities discovered cocaine on board. The aircraft was set on fire with the narcotics still inside and destroyed. It had been put up for sale in January 2013.

25177 02 Series 400B, 25181 01, 25182 03, South African Air Force

An airshow was due to take place in Cape Town to celebrate Republic Day on 31 May 1971, in which it was expected that more than 200 aircraft would take part. On 26 May, the three 125s, known in service as Mercurius Jets, were flying a practice formation prior to the show. The aircraft taking part carried serial Nos 01, 02 and 03. They had made a low pass over the airport and were flying in a V-formation towards the slope of Table Mountain towards an area known as Devil's Peak, located about 5.6 miles (9km) west of the airport and standing at a height of 3,280ft (1,000m). Table Mountain, as is often the case, was covered in cloud. Unfortunately, the three aircraft flew into the mountain and were lost in what was, by any standards, a bizarre accident. All three aircraft were totally destroyed, and the 11 crew members were killed. Thus, of the four original aircraft that had been delivered, only one remained. Replacement aircraft were purchased and, after some years of service, were later transferred to the civil market.

25246 G-AYOJ/9Q-COH/G-AYOJ/G-LORI Series 403B

This aircraft began life as the Hawker Siddeley demonstrator and then spent some time on the register of Zaire (now the Democratic Republic of the Congo) before returning to the UK. It was registered on 15 August 1983 to a company called Re-Enforce Trading Co., based in London. The aircraft had been leased by a Nigerian politician for use in an election campaign in his home country. However, he ultimately failed to pay the lease costs and a full repossession order had been issued by the UK court. G-LORI had been left outside at Lagos International Airport for several months and required work to put it back into full flying condition for the flight back to the UK. Knowing it was unlikely the Nigerian government would simply release the aircraft, the company hired a British pilot, Michael Howard, to collect it. On 19 May 1984, the aircraft was flown out of the airport in Nigeria without a flight plan being filed and with no communication with ATC. It was chased by a Nigerian Air Force Alpha Jet, but the pilot was able to shake off his pursuer by flying very low between the tankers, which were anchored in the Gulf of Guinea. He was then told by Ghana ATC to land there, but he refused and continued to Abidjan, the principal city of Ivory Coast, where he was subsequently put under house arrest. He was later released and returned to the UK, but despite the repossession order, the aircraft was taken back to Nigeria and never flew again. Its registration was not cancelled until 23 February 1993. The pilot explains the complete story in his book, *Never Answer to a Whistle*.

256043 G-BCUX Series 600B

The aircraft was about to make a demonstration flight from the Hawker Siddeley site at Dunsfold on 20 November 1975 with two pilots and seven passengers on board. As it began its take-off run from Runway 07, with its landing and navigation lights operating, a flock of birds was seen to rise from the area towards the northern end of the runway, disturbed as an incoming Harrier aircraft taxied along the perimeter track. The birds rose into the air in quite a dense formation and turned south, just as the

125 became airborne. As this was happening, just before the halfway point of the runway, the captain reduced the power slightly and asked for the undercarriage to be raised. When it was at a height of between 50ft and 100ft and a speed of 150 knots, the aircraft hit the flock of birds. The captain heard and felt a series of bangs as the birds impacted the aircraft. Ground witnesses described hearing several noises, sounding like muffled explosions, and seeing what appeared to be balls of flames from the rear of the engines. Some witness believed they saw birds falling away from the aircraft.

Neither pilot noticed any instrument indications following the bird strike, but the captain did sense an immediate decrease in acceleration, which he believed was due to a loss of power on both engines, after trying to increase the power by re-opening the throttles. He therefore decided to make a forced landing and asked for the undercarriage to be extended and full flaps set. He simultaneously closed the throttles and put the aircraft into full landing mode. The aircraft touched down about 600ft (180m) before the end of the runway. After lowering the nosewheel onto the ground, he applied and maintained full brakes throughout the landing run.

The aircraft then overran the end of the end of the runway, continuing in a straight line across grass fields and through hedges before hitting a ditch on the west side of the nearby main road, about 935ft (285m) beyond the end of the runway. The impact with the ditch damaged the entire undercarriage, completely detaching it from the aircraft. In the process of crossing the road, the aircraft unfortunately struck and demolished a passing car, killing all six occupants. Shortly before the aircraft came to a stop, the captain switched off the high-pressure fuel cocks. Noticing there was light behind him, the captain believed there was the possibility of a fire and immediately ordered an evacuation. As soon as the aircraft came to a halt, the forward entry door was opened, and the aircraft was safely evacuated before the fire spread. The aircraft was consumed by fire and written off. The captain was John Cunningham, known for his wartime exploits as 'Cat's Eyes' Cunningham. He remained as chief test pilot at Hawker Siddeley (Hatfield) until 1978 when BAe was formed.

256036 G-BBRT Series 600B

On 5 April 1974, during the production phase at the Chester factory, the fuselage of this aircraft was being lifted by an overhead crane, so it could be repositioned in another part of the factory. During this process, one of the shackles broke, the fuselage dropped from the crane and was damaged beyond repair. It is believed the damaged unit was later used for paint trials. The fuselage was later moved to helicopter operator Bristow's facility in Redhill, Surrey, with the intention of using it to carry out trials into how its -700 aircraft could be adapted to take its Gnome helicopter engines to various parts of the world.

The aircraft had already been allocated to a customer, Globtik Tankers Ltd, and a registration had been issued. A similar aircraft, c/n 256029, was allocated in its place, but Globtik never took delivery, and the aircraft was eventually delivered to Pertamina Oil Services of Indonesia as PK-PJE.

257062 6V-AIM Series 700B

On 5 September 2015 the aircraft, operated by Senegalair, was flying a medical evacuation sortie from Ouagadougou, Burkina Faso to Dakar, Senegal, a distance of approximately 1,086 miles (1,738km). On board was a French patient; in addition, the plane was carrying two Senegalese nurses and a Senegalese doctor as well as a Congolese engineer and two Algerian crew members. The aircraft climbed to its normal cruising height of 34,000ft (10,363m), but requested a further climb to 38,000ft (11,582m) to avoid a cloud build-up and turbulence. This did not solve the problem, so the aircraft returned to its previous cruising altitude but was allowed to deviate 10nm (19km) from its original track by ATC to avoid the turbulence. At the same time, a Boeing 737-800, 3C-LLY, belonging to Ceiba Intercontinental, based in Malabo, Equatorial Guinea, was operating a scheduled flight, CEL 71, from Dakar to Malabo, with a scheduled stop in Cotonou, Benin. The aircraft was flying at 35,000ft (10,668m).

The aircraft crossed paths with the 125 at 1812hrs, between reporting points DEMOL and GATIL. At 1815hrs, CEL 71 contacted the controller at Dakar Centre, stating they had observed descending traffic from the opposite direction, passing their altitude just behind them. Initially the crew referred to the event as a 'near-miss collision'. The Dakar control centre then attempted to contact the 125, but there was no response. A few minutes later CEL 71 contacted Dakar again, stating they believed the aircraft referred to had touched their wing, but they were not having any problems with controlling the aircraft. The crew decided to omit the scheduled stop at Cotonou and continue directly to Malabo. An inspection at Malabo determined that about 3ft (1m) of the top part of the starboard winglet had broken off.

Dakar made several unsuccessful attempts to contact the 125, though from the radar traces they could see the aircraft had passed over Dakar and was heading towards the sea. The 125 then began to descend and was last seen passing 12,600ft (3,657m) before disappearing from the radar, about 59nm (109km) from Dakar. Subsequent investigations revealed the 125 had been involved in a number of 'level-busting' incidents – flying at the incorrect altitude – during the months leading up to the accident. On the day of the accident, the crew had twice been asked to correct their altitude. It is believed that a problem with the altimeter was the root cause of the accident. Despite a search and rescue mission taking place, no trace of the aircraft or its occupants was ever found.

257178 4W-ACM/G-BMYX/VH-LMP/N700CJ/N621S/EI-COV/N178WB/N803BF/N175MC/ N326TD. Series 700B, later converted to Series A

When this 'B' Series aircraft left Chester for delivery to its first owners, the Yemen-based Shaher Trading Company, in 1982, no one could have imagined its fate. It became the property of BAe when it was traded in by Shaher for a new -800 Series in 1986 and re-registered as G-BMYX and used as a demonstrator, including a brief lease to J C Bamford (JCB), the construction equipment company, while it awaited the delivery of a new aircraft. After a period with Pacific Aviation (Pty) in Australia, it was then transferred to BAe, Inc. in the US, where it was converted to a Series 'A' and used as a demonstrator, before passing through several further hands until finally being registered as N326TD. It was then bought by the Double D Transport Company of Shreveport, Louisiana, on 30 July 2013. On 4 January 2022, David D DeBerardinis was given a prison sentence for a multi-million-dollar wire fraud (a crime that involves electronic communication, for example email or text messages, with the intention of defrauding someone). The aircraft was seized as part of his assets and sold at auction by the United States Secret Service on 11 September 2019, when it was registered to John D Pappas of Cave Junction, Oregon. It was next seen on 18 December 2020 at Campeche in southeastern Mexico. The following day, its wreckage was found by the Guatemalan Army in the Parque Nacional Sierra del Lacandón, near the border with Mexico. Records showed that on 3 December 2020, the aircraft had been sold to R C Lopez in Mexico. Of the crew, one was killed and two were seriously injured.

257184 9K-AGA Series 700B 257187 9K-AGB

The aircraft were originally delivered to Kuwait Airways in 1983 and were used for training and occasional ambulance work and VIP flights. In early August 1990, Kuwait was invaded by Iraq. Both aircraft were taken from Kuwait Airport by Iraqi forces and flown to Baghdad. They were painted in full Iraqi Airways colours, with 9K-AGA being re-registered as YI-AKG and 9K-AGB as YI-AKH. It is believed that YI-AKG was hidden in a remote location near to a palace owned by Saddam Hussein so that, if required, he could use the aircraft to escape from Iraq. After the war, the aircraft was recovered and flown initially to Kuwait with its undercarriage down, to be assessed for further operations. It was later flown to Magec, a fixed-base operator at Luton Airport, where it arrived on 14 December 1994. Some of the relevant documentation had been destroyed during an air raid on Baghdad Airport, so a considerable amount of detective work was required to carry out the necessary work to put the aircraft back into full airworthy condition. It was returned to Kuwait Airways in October 1991 and stayed in the fleet for another three years, before eventually being sold on to Russia; at the time of writing, it is believed to still be in service. The second aircraft, 9K-AGB, was less fortunate, having been destroyed during an allied air strike on Baghdad's main airport in February 1991, during the Gulf War.

258007 G-GAEL Series 800B

This aircraft was bought on 17 November 1983 by Gerald Ronson, the man who brought the concept of self-fuelling to petrol stations to the UK under the brand of Heron International Ltd. On 23 September 1984, the aircraft was involved in a wheels-up landing at Gander Airport Newfoundland, following an otherwise uneventful inbound flight. The aircraft was making a refuelling stop prior to a direct flight to Luton. As the aircraft taxied out, it appeared there was an abnormal tendency for the aircraft to pull to the right. The crew assumed it was caused either by the crosswind or a camber on the surface of the taxiway. Take-off was normal and a rate of climb was established, during which it was noted that when the undercarriage was raised, the main undercarriage lights were extinguished, but the nosewheel indicator remained red.

Additionally, there was an unusual noise from the nosewheel area. Upon reaching a safe altitude, the undercarriage was recycled, but to no avail. The captain cancelled the flight plan and told ATC that he would remain in the area and try to sort out the problem. Further attempts were made to recycle the undercarriage, and two flypasts of the control tower were made, whereupon ATC confirmed that while the nosewheel doors were open, the undercarriage was only partly extended. A decision was taken to make a wheels-up landing once the aircraft had burnt off some fuel to reduce the landing weight. Three practice approaches were made, followed by a touchdown, following which the engines were set to idle and the flaps raised to 15°. The aircraft slid for approximately 2,400ft (730m) before coming to a halt. No one was injured in the incident, and a team was despatched from BAe to effect repairs for the aircraft to allow it to be flown to Chester. Following this, the aircraft suffered from regular fuel leaks, a legacy from the wheels-up landing, which took a long time to identify and repair. It was later taken on charge by Corporate Jets and used as a demonstrator.

Such was Gerald Ronson's faith in the aircraft that he bought a second 125, G-GEIL c/n 258021 (his wife's name was Gail, but he had already used that registration on a Cessna 550), which was delivered on 31 January 1985. In August 1990, he was convicted of false accounting and theft in connection with the Guinness share-dealing scandal of the 1980s and fined £5 million. He served six months of a 12-month prison sentence at Ford Open Prison in West Sussex. The aircraft was sold in February 1991. Gerald Ronson was appointed Commander of the Order of the British Empire (CBE), upon release of the 2012 New Year Honours List in recognition of his later charity work.

258112 OK-1 Series 800B, Botswana Government

On 7 August 1988, a Botswana Air Wing BAe 125-800 was intercepted by a MiG-23 (NATO reporting name: Flogger) while on a flight between Gaborone, Botswana's capital, and Luanda. At the time, it was carrying the president of Botswana and eight other passengers on an official government flight at 35,000ft (10,668m) over Angola. For reasons still unknown, the Angolan interceptor fired a missile,

Below is a brief summary of the types that were built, together with a brief detail of each type.

Designation	Features
Series 1	First version, powered by 3,000lb static thrust (0.0294kN) Viper 20 or 520 engines. Ten built, comprising two prototypes and eight production aircraft.
Series 1A/1B	Upgraded Bristol Siddeley Viper 521 or 522 engines with 3,100lb static thrust (0.0304kN) each, and five cabin windows instead of six. Series 1A for US FAA certification (62 built), Series 1B for sale in the rest of the world. A total of 78 aircraft.
Series 2	Navigation trainer for the RAF (20 built), with the service designation Dominie T1. Powered by Rolls-Royce Viper 301 engines.
Series 3A/B	Powered by an improved Viper 522-powered variant with an increased take-off weight of 21,700lb (9,843kg). Two Series 3, 13 Series 3A and 15 Series 3B for non-US sale were built, totalling 30 aircraft.
Series 3A/RA and 3B/RA	The Series 3 had a MTOW of 22,800lb and an extra 112-gal (509-lit) ventral tank. Twenty Series 3A/RA and 14 Series 3B/RA for non-US sale were built, totalling 34 aircraft.
Series 400A and 400B	This series had increased maximum weights and an outward-opening main entry door. (This had previously opened upwards and inwards.) From 1970, the Series 400A aircraft built for the US market were sold as the Beechcraft Hawker BH125 Series 400A. Sixty-nine of this type were built, with 48 being produced for other markets. Total sales were 117 aircraft.
Series 401 and 403B	Increased maximum weights over the 400A and B.
HS125 CC.1	The RAF designation for Series 400 communication aircraft.
Series 600A and 600B	Equipped with Rolls-Royce Viper 601-22 engines, allowing increased weights and operating speeds. A 3ft 1in (94cm) fuselage stretch, allowing increased passenger capacity. Increased fuel capacity and improved aerodynamics. Note: from 1976, the 600A was marketed as the Beechcraft Hawker 125 Series 600A. Thirty-five were built for the US market and 35 for non-US customers, totalling 70 aircraft.
HS125 CC.2	RAF designation for Series 600 aircraft used for communications.
Series 700A and B	Fitted with Honeywell TFE731-3RH turbofan engines, each producing 3,720lb of static thrust (0.0364kN). The first flight of the new model was on 19 June 1976. The MTOW was increased to 25,500lb (11,567kg). A total of 215 aircraft were sold: 151 of Series 700A and 64 Series 700B.

Civil Designation	Features
BAe 125-800	Contemporary design concept, with Increased wingspan, streamlined nose, extended tailfin, increased fuel capacity and improved engines. First flight: 26 May 1983.
Hawker 800	The final variant of the 125-800 Series. More than 270 of this type were produced. It was replaced by the Hawker 800XP.
Hawker 800XP	Fitted with uprated Honeywell TFE731-5BR1H turbofan engines, with 4,660lb of static thrust (0.045 kN). Also fitted with winglets.
Hawker 800SP	Specific designation for standard Hawker 800 aircraft, retrofitted with Aviation Partners, Inc. (API) winglets.
Hawker 900XP	Hawker 800XP variant, with Honeywell TFE731-50R turbofan engines for increased hot and high performance and longer range. Also fitted with modified avionics.
Hawker 750	A derivative of the Hawker 800XP with a lightweight interior and baggage pannier replacing the rear ventral fuel tank.
BAe 125 Series 1000A and 1000B	The intercontinental version of the Series 800, fitted with Pratt & Whitney Canada PW-305 turbofans 5,200lb static thrust each, plus a 2ft 9in (0.84m) fuselage stretch and an added window on each side, to increase potential passenger capacity to 15. Increased fuel capacity. First flight: 16 June 1990. Fifty-two examples built.
Hawker 1000	New designation after 1994.

Military Designation	Features
Dominie T1	Series 2. RAF training designation.
Mercurius	Series 400B. South African Air Force – used for VIP and communications flights.
CC.1/1A	400B – later F400B. Used by the RAF for VIP and communications.
CC.2/A	600B – later F600B. As above.
CC.3	700B – used by the RAF for VVIP (royal family) and VIP transport.
C-29A	800A USAF – later FAA. Used for flight inspection.
CF-X later U-125	800B Japan Self-Defense Force. Used for flight inspection.
HS-X later U-125A	800A Japan Self-Defense Force. Used for search and rescue.
VC	The prefix used by the Brazilian Air Force for its 125s used for communications and VIP flights.
EU	Aircraft used for utility purposes carried this prefix.
VU	As above.
EC	Used as a prefix for aircraft equipped to calibrate navigation aids.

Bibliography

Aviation Safety Network (online), www. https://aviation-safety.net/database/databases.php

Gunston, Bill, *Hawker: The Story of the 125*, Airworthy Publications International (1996)

Rzjets (online), www.http://rzjets.net/aircraft/

32 Sqn (VIP) operated from RAF Northolt near London. ZE396 was a -700 that operated with the squadron between 1983 and 2015 and is now believed to be buried underground in the Netherlands. (Gerry Manning)

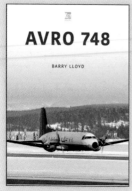

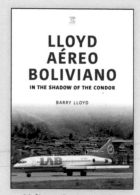